# THE NINETY-NINE BEAUTIFUL NAMES OF GOD

OTHER TITLES IN THE ISLAMIC TEXTS SOCIETY
AL-GHAZĀLĪ SERIES

FROM THE *Iḥyā' ʿulūm al-dīn*

Al-Ghazālī on Invocations & Supplications

Al-Ghazālī on the Manners Relating to Eating

Al-Ghazālī on the Lawful and the Unlawful

Al-Ghazālī on Disciplining the Soul & Breaking the Two Desires

Al-Ghazālī on Patience & Thankfulness

Al-Ghazālī on Love, Longing, Intimacy & Contentment

Al-Ghazālī on Intention, Sincerity & Truthfulness

Al-Ghazālī on Vigilance & Self-Examination

Al-Ghazālī on the Remembrance of Death & the Afterlife

OTHER WORKS

Al-Ghazālī Letter to a Disciple
(*Ayyuhā'l-walad*)

# AL-GHAZĀLĪ

# THE NINETY-NINE BEAUTIFUL NAMES OF GOD · *al-Maqṣad al-asnā fī sharḥ asmā' Allāh al-ḥusnā*

translated with Notes by

DAVID B. BURRELL
and NAZIH DAHER

THE ISLAMIC TEXTS SOCIETY

First published in 1992 by
The Islamic Texts Society
Miller's House
Kings Mill Lane
Great Shelford
Cambridge CB22 5EN, U.K.

Reprint 1995, 1997, 1999, 2004, 2007, 2011,
2012, 2013, 2014, 2015

British Library Cataloguing-in-Publication Data.
A catalogue record for this book is
available from the British Library.

ISBN 978 0946621 30 9 cloth
ISBN 978 0946621 31 6 paper

# CONTENTS

Preface VII

᪄

## THE NINETY-NINE BEAUTIFUL
## NAMES OF GOD

Aim of the Book 1
Beginning of the Book 2

# PREFACE

We present this translation of al-Ghazālī's treatise on the ninety-nine beautiful names of God as a way of allowing those hitherto unfamiliar with Islamic thought to taste something of the reflective capacities of a man who has continued to be recognized as a philosophical theologian over the centuries. The treatise is based in practice: the custom on the part of Muslims to recite the names of God culled from the Qur'ān in a traditional order, usually using a set of 33 beads (*subḥa*) to assist them in enumerating the names. These names recall the attributes whereby God has made Himself known in revelation, and which also connect human expression with matters divine. So to recall God as 'the merciful One' is to allude to those verses of the Qur'ān where God is so named, as well as experiences of mercy we may have had. The connection between our experience and the reality of God's mercy may be tenuous, but the verbal connection provides a slender thread, at least, so that reciting these divine names allows us to bring God into our ambit. Yet the fact that names are more than attributes, because God uses them of Himself in revealing Himself to the Prophet, saves our recitation from reducing God to our experience.

Such at least is the strategy which Ghazālī takes in offering this commentary on a practice. Part One canvasses some of the conceptual issues involved, such as differentiating name from attribute, outlining what is involved in the act of naming, and how names relate to the objects they purport to name. His reflections here mirror some of the issues currently debated in philosophical circles, to show that these matters defy easy resolution. Part Two addresses each name in the traditional list (of Abū Hurayra), first noting how our use of the term to attribute certain features to God may be clarified and purified so as to provide a helpful, rather than a misleading, pointer to the reality which the Qur'ān names in God. The second part of his treatment of each name is normally introduced by the term 'Counsel' (*tanbīh*), and intends to offer counsel on how individual believers might themselves have a share in this divine attribute, and thereby make themselves more pleasing to God. An epilogue to this section explores diverse explanations of this sharing in the attributes of God, and Ghazālī's own positions regarding the Sufi tradition are clarified; while chapters 2 and 3 relate his treatment to a traditional religious ordering of the names as well as to philosophers' views on the divine nature. Part Three inquires about names not found in the traditional list but present in the Qur'ān (or in subsequent tradition), the benefits of enumerating the names in their traditional order, and the relative freedom which believers may enjoy in adding names to those given by God Himself.

Abū Ḥāmid al-Ghazālī (1058-1111) has been credited with establishing a fruitful rapport between Sufism and traditional Islam (*sunna.*) He made his own intellectual and spiritual journey available to us (see McCarthy in bibliography) so that one can grasp the role which Sufi writings played in his own life, as well as the time he spent in seclusion to devote himself to Sufi devotional practices. His relation to this spiritual movement seems to the reader to be more intellectual than that of a thoroughgoing 'seeker', however, and many have remarked that he nowhere speaks of having a master—a decisive criterion for authentic Sufi 'seekers'. Whatever we make of this, there is no doubt that his debt to Sufism is great, and that this work intends to register it explicitly. For the recitation of the names of God, indeed their continual repetition, was a ritual dear to Sufis, as a way of allowing the word of God to penetrate to their hearts. So the very structure of Ghazālī's treatise, as well as some of the specific reflections, displays the practice of this tradition.

We have fixed on the summary works of Anawati-Gardet and of Annemarie Schimmel to supply background for his Sufi references. Daniel Gimaret's *Les noms divins en Islam* appeared while the manuscript was being prepared for publication, so we have added references to it where appropriate. Anyone spurred on by this work to explore the range of commentary on the 'beautiful names of God', will be amply rewarded by Gimaret's comprehensive treatment, which links Ghazālī's work with predecessors and successors to mine a rich vein of Islamic thought and life.

The critical text of Fadlou Shehadi has served as the basis of our translation, as well as providing references for the *ḥadīths* which Ghazālī cites: by author, book and section numbers from the standard works—where these could be identified. Our procedure was to meld independent renderings after considerable discussion, assisted by lexical works like Jabre and Kazimirski. We are especially grateful to Fadlou Shehadi for his scrutiny of our version of Part One, although we wish to assume full responsibility for whatever infelicities may mar this translation. A special word of thanks to Cheryl Reed, whose devoted attention to version after version assured an error-free final text. We are indebted to the Islamic Texts Society for an initial grant, which allowed us to establish a summer's intensive working pattern, as a model for our collaborative efforts through the academic year 1987-88. Moreover, the hospitality of Aisha and Faarid Gouverneur, and of Batul Salazar, together with the assistance of Timothy Winter, in Cambridge during July 1989, proved invaluable to bringing this work to term—however incomplete one always feels that to be when attempting to render faithfully the thought of another.

With a few exceptions, we have accepted as English equivalents for the Names the rendering offered in Titus Burckhardt, *Mirror of the Intellect* (Cambridge: Quinta Essentia, 1987). We have followed standard rules for transliteration. We have been helped, in identifying *ḥadīth* references, beyond those traced by

Shehadi, by a recent edition of the text completed as a dissertation at al-Azhar University in Cairo by ʿĪsā ʿAbdullāh ʿAlī, in the Faculty of Doctrine and Philosophy (Cairo: Dār al-Muṣṭafā, 1988). We have included Shehadi's references to *al-Mughnī ʿan ḥaml al-asfār*, by ʿAbd al-Raḥīm b. al-Ḥusayn al-ʿIrāqī, which appears in the lower half of the pages of Ghazālī's *Iḥyāʾ ʿulūm al-dīn* (Cairo, 1928), as a way of identifying *ḥadīth* which appear in the *Iḥyāʾ* as well as in this work. Terms or names which become common coinage, like *ḥadīth* or our author al-Ghazālī, are anglicized after their initial use, as are the abbreviations for recurring references noted in the bibliography. Page references to Shehadi's critical text appear in brackets in our text.

# THE NINETY-NINE BEAUTIFUL NAMES OF GOD

## AIM OF THE BOOK [11]

*In the Name of God the Infinitely Good, the Merciful*

PRAISE BE TO GOD, alone in His majesty and His might, and unique in His sublimity and His everlastingness, who clips the wings of intellects well short of the glow of His glory, and who makes the way of knowing Him pass through the inability to know Him; who makes the tongues of the eloquent fall short of praising the beauty of His presence unless they use the means by which He praises Himself, and use His names and attributes which He has enumerated. And may blessings be upon Muḥammad, the best of His creatures, and on his companions and his family.

Now, a brother in God—great and glorious—to answer whom is a religious duty, has asked me to elucidate the meanings of the most beautiful names of God. His questions were incessant, and made me take one step forward and another backward, hesitating between heeding his inquiry and so satisfying the duty of brotherliness, or declining his request by following the way of caution and deciding not to venture into danger, for human powers fall far short of attaining this goal.

How else could it be? For two things deter a discerning person from plunging into such a sea. First of all, the matter itself represents a lofty aspiration, difficult to attain and uncertain of accomplishment. For it is at the highest summit and represents the farthest of goals, such that minds are bewildered by it and the sight of intellects falls far short of its principles, not to mention its farthest reaches. How could human powers follow the way of investigation and scrutiny regarding the divine attributes? Can the eyes of bats tolerate the light of the sun? [12]

The second deterrent: declaring the essence of the truth of this matter all but contradicts whatever the collectivity has hitherto believed. Now weaning creatures from their habits and familiar beliefs is difficult, and the threshold of truth is too exalted to be broached by all or to be sought after except by lone individuals. The nobler the thing sought after the less help there is. Whoever mixes with people is right to be cautious; but it is difficult for one who has seen the truth to pretend not to have seen it. For one who does not know God—great and glorious—silence is inevitable, while for one who knows God most high, silence is imposed. So it is said: 'for one who knows God, his tongue is dulled'. But the sincerity of the original request, together with its persistence, overcame these excuses. So I asked God—great and glorious—to facilitate what is right and be liberal in rewarding by His graciousness and His benevolence and His abundant generosity; for He is the liberal and generous One, indulgent to His servants.

## THE BEGINNING OF THE BOOK [13]

We have seen fit to divide the discussion in this book into three parts. Part One will treat preliminary and introductory matters; Part Two, goals and objectives; Part Three supplementary and complementary matters. The chapters of the first part will consider the goals in an introductory and preparatory way, while the chapters of the third part are attached to them so as to complement and complete them. But the core of what we are seeking is contained in the middle part.

As for the first part, it includes (1) explaining the truth of what is to be said concerning the name, the named, and the act of naming, (2) exposing the errors into which most groups have fallen regarding this matter, and (3) clarifying whether it is permitted for those names of God which are close to one another in meaning—like *al-ʿAẓīm* (the Immense), *al-Jalīl* (the Majestic), and *al-Kabīr* (the Great)—to be predicated according to a single meaning so that they would be synonymous, or must their meanings differ? Furthermore, (4) it explains about a single name which has two meanings: how does it share these two meanings? Is it predicated of both of them, as a general predicate of the things it names [as 'animal' is said of a lion and a lamb], or must it be predicated of one of them in particular? Finally, (5) it explains how man shares in the meaning of each of the names of God—great and glorious.

The second part includes (1) the clarification of the meaning of the ninety-nine names of God and (2) the explanation how the people of the Sunna reduce them all to an essence with seven attributes, and (3) how the doctrine of the Muʿtazilites and the philosophers reduces them to a single essence without multiplicity. [14]

The third part explains (1) that the names of God most high exceed the ninety-nine by divine instruction, and explains (2) how it is permissible to describe God most high by whatever may qualify Him even if no permission or divine instruction be found—so long as it is not prohibited. Finally, it explains (3) the advantage of the enumeration and specification of the one hundred-minus-one names.

# PART ONE

## CHAPTER ONE

## On showing the meaning of the name, the named and the naming

MANY have plunged into the matter of the name and the thing named, and taken different directions, and most of the groups have deviated from the truth. Some say (A) that the name is the same as the thing named, but other than the act of naming, while others say (B) the name is other than the thing named, but the same as the act of naming. Still a third group, known for its cleverness in constructing arguments and in polemics [*kalām*], claims (C) that the name (C.1) can be the same as the thing named, as we say of God most high that He is essence and existent; and that the name can also be other than the thing named, as in our saying that God is creator and provider. For these indicate creating and providing, which are other than Him. So it can be such that the name (C.2) may not be said either to be the same as the thing named or other than it, as when we say 'knowing' and 'powerful': both refer to knowing and power, yet attributes of God cannot be said to be the same as God or other than Him.

Now the dispute (A, B) comes down to two points: (1) whether or not the name is the same as the act of naming, and (2) whether or not the name is identical with the thing named. The truth is that the name is different from both the act of naming and the thing named, and that those three terms are distinct and not synonymous. There is no way to show the truth of this matter without explaining the meaning of each one of the three words separately, and then explaining what we mean when we say: 'x is the same as y' or 'x is other than y'. For this is the method of uncovering the truth in such things, and whoever departs from this method will not succeed at all.

For every asserted knowing—that is, whatever is susceptible of assertion or denial—is without doubt a proposition consisting of a subject [qualified] and a predicate [quality], and the relation of predicate to the subject. So it is inevitable that knowledge of the subject and its definition precede the assertion by way of conceiving [18] its definition and its essential reality, followed by the knowledge of the predicate and its definition by way of conceiving its definition and its essential reality, and then attending to the relation of this predicate to the subject: whether it exists in it or is denied of it. For whoever wants to know, for example, whether angels are eternal or created must first know the meaning of the word 'angel', then the meaning of 'eternal' and 'created', and then determine whether to affirm or deny one of the two predicates of 'angel'. Likewise, there is no escape from knowing the meaning of 'name' and of 'thing named', as well as knowing the meaning of identity and difference, so that one may conceivably know whether the name is identical or different from the thing named.[1]

In explaining the definition and essential reality of the name, we say that things have existence as individuals, in speech, or in minds. Existence as individuals is the fundamental real existence, while existence in the mind is cognitional, formal existence; and existence in speech is verbal and indicative. So heaven, for example, has existence in itself as an individual reality; then existence in our minds and souls, because the form of heaven is impressed in our eyes and then in our imagination, so that even if heaven were to disappear, for example, while we survived, the representation of heaven would still be present in our imagination. This representation, moreover, is what is expressed in knowledge, for it is the likeness of the object known since it is similar to it and corresponds to it, much as the image reflected in a mirror is similar to the external form facing it.

As for what exists in speech, it is the word composed of three [19] segmented sounds: the first of which is expressed by [the letter] *sīn*, and second by *mīm*, and the third by *alif*, as when we say *'samā'*'['heaven']. Our saying indicates what is in the mind, and what is in the mind is a representation of that which exists, which corresponds to it. For if there were no existence in individuals, there would be no form impressed on the mind, and if there were no form impressed on the mind and no man conscious of it, it would not be expressed in speech. So the word, the knowledge, and the object known are three distinct things, though they mutually conform and correspond; and are sometimes confused by the dull-witted, and one of them may fail to be distinguished from the other.[2]

How could these objects fail to be distinguished from one another, given the properties associated with each of them which are not connected with the other? Insofar as man, for example, exists as an individual, sleeping and waking, living and dead, standing, walking and sitting, are all associated with him. But insofar as man exists in minds, subject and predicate, general and specific, universal and particular, proposition and the like are associated with it. And insofar as man exists in speech, Arabic or Persian or Turkish are associated with it, as well as having many or few letters, and whether it be a noun, a verb, or a particle, and the like. This existence is something which can differ from time to time, and also vary according to the usage of countries, whereas existence in individuals and in the mind never varies with time or with cultures.

If you have understood this, leave aside for the time being the existence which is in individuals and in minds, and attend to existence in speech, for that pertains to our goal. So we say: words consist of segmented letters, posited by human choice to indicate individual things. They are divided into what is posited primarily and what is posited secondarily. [20]

What is posited primarily is like your saying 'heaven', 'tree', 'man', and the like. And what is posited secondarily is like your saying 'noun', 'verb', 'particle', 'command', 'negation', and 'imperfect [tense]'. We have said that these are posited secondarily because the words posited to indicate things are divided into (1) what indicates a meaning in something other than itself, and so is called a particle,[3] and (2) what indicates a meaning in itself. And the latter—what indicates meaning in itself—is divided into (2.1) what indicates the time of the existence of that meaning, and is called a verb—like your saying 'he hit', 'he hits' [or 'he will hit']; and (2.2) what does not indicate time, and is called a noun—like your saying 'heaven' or 'earth'.[4] First of all, words were posited to indicate individuals, after which nouns, verbs and particles were posited to indicate the types of words; because after being posited, words also became existent individuals and their images were formed in minds and so were suited in turn to be indicated by movements of the tongue.

It is conceivable that there be words posited in third and fourth place, so that when nouns are divided into types, and each division is known by a name, that noun will be in the third rank, as when one says, for example, that nouns are divided into indefinite and definite, or some other division. The point of all this is that you understand that the noun goes back to a word that was posited secondarily. So if one says to us: what is the definition of a noun? we say: it is a word posited to indicate; and we might add to that what distinguishes it from particles and verbs. At this time our goal is not to formulate the definition precisely; but simply to show that what is intended by a name is the meaning which is in the third rank, which belongs to speech, leaving aside what is in individuals or in minds.

Now if you understand that the name is simply the word posited for indicating, you should know [21] that everything posited for indicating has a positor, a positing, and the thing posited. The thing posited is called the named, and it is the thing indicated insofar as it is indicated. And the positor is called namer, while the positing is called naming. One says that someone names his son when he posits a word indicating him, and his positing is called naming. The term 'naming' may also be applied to mentioning the name posited, as when one calls a person, saying 'O Zayd!' we say that he named him. But if he said 'O Abu Bakr', we say he named him by his *agnomen*[5] So the term 'naming' is common to positing the name and to mentioning it, although it seems that positing is more deserving of it than mentioning.[6]

Name, naming, and named are analogous to motion, moving, mover, and moved. And these are four different terms which indicate different notions. 'Motion' indicates transition from place to place, while 'moving' refers to the initiation of this motion, and 'mover' to the agent of the motion, while 'moved' indicates the thing in which the motion is, along with its coming forth from the agent—unlike 'the moving one', which refers only to the place in which the motion is and not to the agent. If the meanings of these terms are now clear, let us consider whether it is possible to say about them that they are the same or different from one another.

This question will not be understood, however, unless one knows the meaning of 'different from' [or 'other than'] and 'same as'. Our saying 'is the same as' is used in three ways. One way corresponds to saying 'wine [*khamr*] is wine [*ʿuqār*] or 'lion [*layth*] is lion [*asad*]'. This goes for everything which is one in itself yet has two synonymous names whose meanings in no way differ, neither by addition or subtraction, but only in their letters. Such names are called synonymous. [22]

The second way corresponds to the saying 'the sharp sword [*ṣārim*] is the sword [*sayf*]' or 'the sword made of Indian steel [*muhannad*] is the sword [*sayf*]'. This differs from the first way, for these names differ in meanings and are not synonymous.

For *ṣārim* refers to a sword insofar as it is cutting, and *muhannad* points out the sword's relation to India, while *sayf* refers merely to the thing indicated with no indication of anything else. Only synonymous terms differ simply in their letters and not in any addition or subtraction. So let us call this category 'interlocked', since 'sword' enters into the comprehension of the three terms while some of them indicate something more along with it.

The third way occurs when one says 'snow is white and cold', so that white and cold are one, and white is the same as cold. This is the more far-fetched way, since their unity is due to the unity of the subject posited with the two predicates, meaning that one individual subject is qualified by whiteness and coldness. In short, our saying 'it is the same as' indicates a plurality which is one in some respect. For if there were no unity, one could not say 'it is one with'; and without a plurality there would be no 'it is identical with', for this expression indicates two things.

Let us return to our purpose and say: whoever thinks that the name is the same as the named, by analogy with synonymous terms—as in saying 'wine [*khamr*] is wine [*ᶜuqār*]'—commits a serious error. For the meaning of 'named' is different from the meaning of 'name', as we have shown that the name is a word which indicates, whereas the named is the thing indicated, and it may not even be a word. Furthermore, the name is Arabic or Persian or Turkish, as posited by Arab, Persian, or Turk; whereas the thing named may not be of that sort. In asking about the name, one says 'what is it?', but in asking about the named, one might say: 'who is he?' As when a person is present, we say: 'what is his name?' and someone says 'Zayd'; while if we ask about him, one says: 'who is he?' And if [23] a handsome Turk is named with an Indian name, it will be said that the name is ugly but the one named handsome. Or if he is named with a multi-lettered name, which is burdensome to articulate, it will be said: the name is burdensome yet the one named is light. Furthermore, the name may be a figure of speech, but not the one named. Or the name may be changed in translation, but not the one named. All this should apprise you that the name is other than the thing named. If you ponder, you will find differences other than these, but the discerning one is satisfied with a little and the dull-witted will only be confused by more.

As for the second way, if it is said that the name is the thing named, in the sense that the thing named is derived from the name and enters into it, as 'sword' enters into the meaning of 'sharp sword', then it would be necessary that naming, the namer, the thing named, and the name all be one, because all of them derive from the name, and indicate it. But this is reckless talk; like saying that motion, moving, mover, and moved are one since all are derived from motion—and that is wrong. For 'motion' refers to transition with no indication of the place, agent or action, while 'mover' indicates the agent of motion, and 'moved' the place of motion together with its being acted upon—unlike 'the one that moves', for it refers to the place or motion without indicating its being something acted upon; while 'moving' refers to the action or the movement without any indication of its agent or place. These are different realities, although movement is not extrinsic to any of them.

Motion may be conceived in one way as a reality in itself, or conceived in relation to an agent. But this relationship is not something added, for the relationship is conceived as between two things, and something added is conceived as one with the thing. Furthermore, conceiving its relation to place is not the same as conceiving its relation to an agent. [24] How is that? The relation of motion to place and its requirements is necessary to it, while its relation to an agent is speculative—that is, it requires a judgment regarding the existence of two relations without representation. Similarly, the name has an indication and a thing indicated, which is the thing named, and positing the name is the action of a free agent, and that is the naming. So this interlocking is not like the inclusion of 'sword' in the meaning of 'sharp sword' [*ṣārim*] or of 'sword made of Indian steel' [*muhannad*], because a sharp sword is a sword with an attribute, and the same with *muhannad*, so that 'sword' is contained within them. But the thing named is not a name with an attribute, nor is the act of naming a name with an attribute, so this interpretation does not work here either.

As for the third way, which refers to the unity of the object with a combined property, this again—with its farfetchedness—does not obtain in the name and the named nor in the name and the act of naming, so that it could be said that a single thing is posited in order to be called a name and a naming, as in the example of snow—where one meaning was qualified by cold and white. Neither is it like saying: the faithful one [*al-ṣiddīq*]—may God be pleased with him—is Ibn Abī Quḥāfa[7], because this is to be interpreted that the person who is described as 'faithful' is the same as the one who is related by birth to Abī Quḥāfa. So the expression 'is the same as' signifies the unity of the thing posited while it definitively asserts that there is a difference between the two qualifications. For the meaning of 'the faithful one'—may God be pleased with him—differs from the meaning of filiality to Abū Quḥāfa.

Neither the literal nor the metaphorical interpretations of 'is the same as' come at all close to the relation of name to thing named, or name with the act of naming. The essential reality of the formula ['x is same as y'] resolves to synonymy of names, as in our saying that a lion [*layth*] is a lion [*asad*]—granted that there be no linguistic difference between the meanings of the two words. And if there be a difference between them, let [25] another example be sought. This resolves to the unity of the essential reality with a multiplicity of names. For it is clear that our saying 'is the same as' presupposes multiplicity in one respect and unity in another. The most authentic respect will be that of unity in meaning and multiplicity in words alone. This much should suffice to show how little this long-winded dispute achieves. It has become clear to you that 'name', 'naming', and 'named' are words with different meanings and intentions, so it is proper to say of one of them that it is not the second, and not that it is the same as the second, because 'other than' contrasts with 'same as'.

As for the third position (C), dividing the name into (C.1) what is the same as the named and what differs from it, and (C.2) into what is neither the same nor different, it is farthest from what is right and the most confused of all the positions, unless (C.1) be interpreted as if to say: the name itself was not intended by the name which was divided into three types, but rather the meaning of the name and the thing indicated was intended by that division. But the meaning of the name is other than the name: the meaning of the name is the same as the thing indicated, and the thing indicated is not the indication. And this division, which has already been mentioned, deals with the meaning of the name. For it is right to say: the meaning of the name might be the essence of the thing named and its essential reality and quiddity, and these are (1) names of kinds which are not derived—as when we say 'man', 'knowledge', or 'white'. So far as (2) derived names are concerned, they do not indicate the essential reality of the thing named, but leave it in umbrage, and only indicate an attribute of it—as when we say 'knower' or 'writer'. Then the derived term divides into (2.1) what refers to an attribute of state in the thing named, as in knowing or white; and (2.2) what refers to the relation the attribute has to what is not separate from it as in creator and writer. [26]

The definition of the first kind [i.e., underived nouns] is: every name is said in answer to the question: what is it? Pointing to a human being and saying: what is it? is not like saying: who is it?, since the answer to the first is 'a man'. And if one were to say 'an animal', he would fail to mention that by which it is what it is, because man's quiddity is not constituted by animality alone: man is a man by being a rational animal, not by being an animal alone. The word 'man' means 'rational animal'. If instead of 'man' one were to say 'white' or 'tall' or 'knower' or 'writer', that would not answer the question: what is it? For by 'white' we understand something or other with the attribute of white, without informing what that thing is. Similarly, the meaning of 'knower' is something or another with the attribute of knowledge, while that of 'writer' is something or another with the activity of writing. Of course, it is possible that one understands that a writer is a man, from things extrinsic to the meaning of the word and evidences external to it. Likewise, if one points to a colour and says: what is it?, the answer is that it is whiteness. Were one to use a derived term and say: 'it is radiant' or 'the diffusion of the light to sight', that would not be an answer. For when we say: what is it? we are looking for the reality of the essence, the quiddity by which it is what it is, while 'radiant' is something or other having radiance, and 'diffusion' is something or other which has diffusion.

Furthermore, this distinction concerning the referent of the names and their meanings is sound. It is possible to express it in this way: that the name may refer to the essence and may also refer to what is other than the essence, but that would be taking liberties in applying it. For our saying: 'it refers to what is other than the essence' would not be correct unless it were to be interpreted as our intending to say: 'other than the quiddity expressed in answer to the question 'what is it?' For 'knower' refers to an essence which has knowledge, so it also refers to an essence. There is a difference between saying 'knower' and saying 'knowledge', because 'knower' refers to an essence having knowledge, while the word 'knowledge' does not refer to anything but knowledge. [27]

Saying that the name might be the essence of the thing named has two shortcomings, and both need to be corrected. Either replace 'name' with 'meaning of the name' or replace 'essence' with 'quiddity of the essence'. Then it will be said: the meaning of the name may be the reality of the essence and its quiddity, and it may be other than the essential reality. As for saying that the creator is other than the thing named, two interpretations should be considered: (1) if by creator the word 'creator' is intended, the word is always other than the referent of the word. But if (2) what is intended is that the meaning of the word is other than the thing named, that would be impossible, since 'creator' is a name, and the meaning of every name is the thing it names. For if the thing named were not understood from the name, it would not be its name. 'Creator' is not a name for creation, although creation is contained within it, nor is 'writer' a name for writing—nor is 'the thing named' a name for the act of naming. Rather, 'creator' is the name of an essence in so far as creation originates from it. What is understood from 'creator' is the essence as well, but not the true reality of the essence. What is rather understood is the essence in so far as it has an attribute related to it, as when we say 'father'. The meaning of that term is not the essence of the father, but rather the essence of the father insofar as he is related to a son.

Attributes are divided into relational and not relational, and the thing qualified by all of them is the essence. When one says 'creator', it is an attribute and every attribute is an affirmation, but no affirmation is contained in this word except creation. Yet creation is other than the creator, and no true description of a creator can be derived from creation. For that reason it is said that it ['creator'] refers to what is other than the thing named [viz., creation]. So we believe that the saying: the name makes one understand something other than the thing named, is a contradiction, as though one were to say: the sign makes known something other than the thing signified. But since the thing named is equivalent to the meaning of the name, how can the meaning be other than the thing named, or the thing named other than the meaning? [28]

As for saying that the creator cannot be described from creation, nor the writer from his writing, that is not so. The proof that it can be so described is the fact that sometimes it is described by it and at other times denied of it. Relation is an attribute that can be denied or affirmed of the thing related, as with whiteness, which is not something related. So whoever knows Zayd and Bakr, and also knows that Zayd is Bakr's father, definitely knows something. And this thing which he knows is either an attribute or a subject of attribution. It is not the essence of the subject but rather an attribute. But an attribute does not subsist in itself, but is rather a quality of Zayd. Relations are like attributes to the things related, except that their meanings can only be conceived by comparing two things, but that does not deprive them of the status of attributes.

Now if one were to say that God—great and glorious—is not described by His being creator, that would be unbelief, just as it would be unbelief to say: God is not described by His being a knower. Yet one who says this may fall into such a confusion because the *Mutakallimūn*[8] do not reckon relations among the accidents. So if one asks them: what does 'accident' mean? they say: what exists in a substratum and does not subsist in itself. And if they be asked whether a relation subsists in itself, they would say: no. But if one asked them: is a relation an existent or not? they would say that it is. They cannot say that fatherhood is non-existent, for if it were the case that fatherhood did not exist, there would not be one father in the world. Yet if they were told that fatherhood subsists in itself, they would say: no. So they are obliged to admit that it exists but that it does not subsist in itself; rather it subsists in a substratum. And they acknowledge that 'accident' expresses what is existent in a substratum—but then they turn around and deny that relation is an accident. [29]

The saying (C.2) that some names are said to be neither the thing named nor other than the thing named is also wrong, and that can be shown by the name 'knower'. (And if this [word] be excluded since revelation does not give permission to apply that name to God—great and glorious—one could say: declaring what is true and accurate is not contingent on special permission. So perhaps it can be tolerated now, and one may return to consider man as described by knowledge.)

Would you definitively say that knowledge is not other than man, and that man is an existent while knowledge is not, and that the definition of knowledge is other than the definition of man? For if it were said that knowledge is other than man, yet we say of a single person that he is a knower and a man, then the knower would not be the same as the man nor other than the man, because man is the thing described. But if this were said, we would say that this must also be the case with 'writer', 'carpenter', or 'creator', for the thing described by each of these is a man as well.

The truth requires precision: it should be said that the meaning of the word 'man' is other than the meaning of the word 'knower', since 'man' means 'rational animal' and 'knower' means something or other which has knowledge. Moreover, each of the two terms is other than the other, and the meaning of one differs from that of the other. So in this respect they differ, and it is not possible to say that they are the same, yet in another respect [i.e., sharing the same substratum] they are the same and it is not possible to say that one differs from the other. The latter situation obtains when one considers the single essence which is described by being man and by knowing. What is named by 'man' is what is described by being a knower—as the thing named by 'snow' was the thing described by being cold and white. By this kind of consideration and interpretation, the name is the same as the named, while on the first interpretation it is different. It would contradict reason if on a single interpretation they were neither the same [30] nor different, just as it would be a contradiction were they the same and different—for 'other than' and 'same as' are opposed to each other as are negation and affirmation; there is no middle term between them.[9]

Whoever understands this knows that, if the attributes of power and knowledge are asserted of God—great and glorious—as something added to the essence, then something other than the essence has been asserted, and difference in meaning as well, even though this is not stated in words lest it violate what is laid down in divine instruction. How could it be otherwise? Even if mentioning the definition of knowledge included in it the knowledge of God—great and glorious, it still would not include either His power or His essence. For must not what remains extrinsic to the definition be other than what is included in it? Furthermore, would it not be possible for the one defining knowledge, if power is not included in its definition, to excuse himself and say: what is the harm of excluding power from the definition since the origination of knowledge and of power is other than knowledge itself, and I do not have to include it in the definition of knowledge? Likewise, the essence which knows is other than knowledge, and I do not have to include it in the definition of knowledge. And whoever rejects the saying: the thing included in the definition is other than what is extrinsic to it, and changes the application of the phrase 'other than' here, is one of those who fail to understand the meaning of the term 'other than'. In my opinion, however, it is not that he does not understand, for the meaning of the phrase 'other than' is clear, but he might be saying with his tongue what reason finds offensive and what his insight denies. The aim of demonstrative argument is not to lay hold of speech but minds, so that the truth of the matter is inwardly recognized, whether it be expressed in speech or not.

It might be said that what compelled those who say that the name is the same as the thing named to say just that was a certain wariness, lest they say: the name is a word which indicates by convention. For that would make it necessary for them to say that God—great and glorious—had no name in eternity, since there were no words or speakers, since words are created. We say, however, that this is a slight difficulty, easy to overcome [31], since it can be said: the meanings of names were affirmed eternally, but names were not, because the names are Arabic or Persian, and are all created. And this is the case regarding every word which refers to the meaning of the divine essence or an attribute of that essence—like the Holy One [*al-Quddūs*], which has the attribute of holiness in eternity, or like the Omniscient One [*al-ʿAlīm*], which has been knowing from eternity.

We have already shown that things have three degrees of existence. The first is in individuals, and this existence is qualified by eternity with regard to whatever applies to the essence and the attributes of God—great and glorious. The second degree is in minds, and this is created since minds are created, while the third is in speech and comprises names. This degree is also created in the creation of speech. Indeed, we intend 'the knowledges' by the thing established in minds, and when related to the essence of God—great and glorious—these are eternal, because God—great and glorious—is existent and knowing in eternity, and knows Himself to be existent and knowing. And His existence was affirmed in Himself and also in His knowledge. And the names which He will inspire in His servants and which He creates in their minds and their speech were also known by Him. From this interpretation, it becomes possible to say: there are names in eternity.

As for names which resolve to action, like 'creator' and 'fashioner' and 'bestower', some say He is described as a creator in eternity; yet others say He is not so described. But the disagreement has no basis. For 'creator' is used in two senses: one of them is asserted emphatically from eternity while the other is as emphatically denied—yet there is no way to disagree about them. The sword is named severer while it is in the scabbard, and it is named severer when making an incision in the neck. But in the scabbard it is potentially severer, whereas in making the incision it is a severer actually. So water in a pitcher is quenching but potentially, whereas in the stomach it is actually quenching. The meaning of water's being quenching in the pitcher is that it has the attribute which [32] succeeds in quenching when it encounters the stomach, and this attribute is water-ness. The sword in the scabbard is severer by an attribute which succeeds in cutting when it meets its object, and this attribute is sharpness. And there is no need that the quality be renewed within itself.[10]

The Producer—may He be praised and exalted—is eternally creator in the sense in which water in the pitcher is said to be quenching: by an attribute which succeeds in bringing about action and creation. In the second sense, however, God is not creator eternally: that is, creation is not coming forth from Him. Similarly, He is eternal in the sense that He is named the Omniscient One and the Holy One and so forth. And He is so eternally, whether someone else names Him with such a name or not. Most of the disputants' errors stem from their failure to distinguish the meanings of shared terms, and had such distinctions been made, most of their disagreements would have disappeared.

If it were said: God the most high says: *'Those whom you worship beside Him are but names which you have named, you and your fathers'* (XII:40), though it is known that they did not worship words which were composed of letters, but rather the things named; we say: whoever infers from this [that names are the same as things named] fails to understand its meaning, for He did not say that they worshipped the things named without the names. Moreover, His words clearly state that names are other than the things named. If one says that Arabs were worshippers of the things named without the things named, that would be a contradiction. But if he said: they worshipped the things named without the name, that could be understood without contradiction. Were names the same as the things named, then the latter saying would be like the first.

Then let it be said: what the verse means is that the divine name they gave to idols was a name without there being anything named, because the thing named is the meaning affirmed in reality in so far as something is indicated [33] by a word.

Yet divinity was not affirmed in reality nor was it known in minds; rather its names were existing in speech, but they were names devoid of meaning. Whoever is made happy by being named wise when he is not in fact wise is said to be happy with the name, since there is no meaning behind the name. This is another proof that the name is other than the thing named, because the verse connects the name with the act of naming, and relates the act of naming to those who actively make it their own, as it is said: *'the names which you have named'*, that is, the names resulting from their act of naming and their own activity. For actual idols were not created by their act of naming.

If it were said: God the most high says: *'Praise the name of thy Lord most high'* (LXXXVII:1), yet the essence is what is praised and not the name; we say: the name here is an addition by way of relation, and such things are customary in Arabic. It is like His saying: *'Naught is as His likeness'* (XLII:11). It is not possible to infer from this that a likeness is affirmed of Him just because He said: *'naught is as His likeness'*—as there is an affirmation of son in the saying: 'no one is like his son'. Rather the 'as' in the verse is redundant.

This is not very different from addressing the one named by a name exalting him, as when a distinguished person is addressed by the honorific: 'your honour' and 'your counsel', and one says: 'peace be upon his blessed honour and noble counsel'. The aim was to salute him—'peace be upon him'—but he is addressed by something which pertains to him in a certain way, by way of exaltation. Likewise, although the name is other than the thing named, nevertheless it pertains to it and corresponds with it—and this need not obscure the principles of positing for someone who is clear-sighted. [34]

How is that? Those who say that the name is other than the thing named have demonstrated that from His saying: *'Allah's are the fairest names'* (VII:180), and from the saying of the Prophet—may God's blessing and peace be upon him—that 'God the most high has ninety-nine names—one hundred minus one—and whosoever enumerates them will enter into paradise'.[11] They also say: were He the thing named, there would be ninety-nine things named, but that is impossible, because the thing named is one. Here they were forced to acknowledge that the name is other than the thing named, but they said: it is possible that it convey the meaning of the act of naming and not the meaning of the thing named. Others have admitted that the name might convey the meaning of the thing named, even though in principle it is other than the thing named. In support of this, His saying was revealed to them: *'Praise the name of thy Lord most high'* (LXXXVII:1), but neither one of the parties was able to draw conclusions or respond to it at all.

As for His saying: *'Praise the name of thy Lord most high'*, we had already mentioned what was relevant concerning it. In response to this reasoning, they answered that the thing named is one, yet what is intended by 'name' right here is the act of naming. But that is wrong on two counts. First, when one says that the name is the same as the thing named, he should go on to say that the thing named is in this case ninety-nine, because the sense of 'the thing named' is the meaning of the name, according to the one speaking. The meaning of the Omniscient is other than the meaning of the Powerful, the Holy, the Creator, and the rest. Each name has a meaning signifying its proper condition, even though all resolve to qualifying one essence. Whoever says that sounds as if he is saying: the name is the same as the meaning. He also might say: 'the beautiful meanings of God the most high', for the things named are meanings, and of course there are many of them.

Secondly, their saying that what is intended by 'name' here is the act of naming can be seen to be wrong from our explanation [35] that the act of naming is mentioning the name or positing it. For the act of naming increases and multiplies with an increase in the namers, even when there is but one name—just as the mention and knowledge multiply with the multiplicity of those who mention and who know, even though the thing mentioned or known is but one. Many acts of naming do not demand many names because that expression refers to the actions of those who name. I do not intend by 'names' here acts of naming, but I rather intend names. For names are words posited to indicate different meanings, so there is no need for this arbitrariness in interpretation, whether the name is said to be the same as the thing named or not.

This much should suffice to elucidate this question, which is of so little use that it hardly deserves this long elaboration. Our goal in this explication is rather to teach methods for exploring discussions like these, so that they may be directed to those asking questions more important than these. For the consideration of these questions mostly concerns words rather than meanings. But God knows best.

CHAPTER TWO [36]

# Explanation of names close to one another in meaning, and whether it is possible that they be synonyms indicating only one meaning, or must their meanings differ?

THOSE WHO have plunged into an explanation of such names have not attended to this matter, and have not dismissed [the possibility] that two names indicate but one meaning—as in 'the Great' [*al-Kabīr*] and 'the Tremendous' [*al-ʿAẓīm*], or 'the Powerful' [*al-Qadīr*] and 'the Determiner' [*al-Muqtadir*], or 'the Creator' [*al-Khāliq*] and 'the Producer' [*al-Bāri'*]. I consider this highly unlikely, whichever two names be taken from the set of ninety-nine. For a name is not intended for its letters but for its meaning, and synonymous names differ only in their letters. Indeed the merit of these names is in the meanings which underlie them, for should you withhold meaning, only the utterance would remain; and a meaning indicated by a thousand names is hardly better than a meaning indicated by one name. Moreover, it is improbable that this limited enumeration be made perfect through repeating words with a single meaning; it is rather more likely that a specific meaning underlie each word.

For when we notice two words close to each other in meaning, one of two things must obtain. First, we could explain that one of them is outside the ninety-nine—as is the case with 'the One' [*al-Aḥad*] and 'the Unique' [*al-Wāḥid*]. 'The Unique' appears in the well-known account passed down by Abū Hurayra—God be pleased with him. Yet in another account, 'the One' appears instead of 'the Unique'. What completes the enumeration, however, will be the meaning of God's unity [*tawḥīd*], whether conveyed by the expression 'the Unique' or 'the One'. For it is highly improbable that these two expressions hold the place of two names when their meaning is one. Second, one could take upon oneself the task of showing the distinct nature [37] of one word over the other by showing that it includes an indication that the other does not. For example, were a text to mention 'the Forgiver' [*al-Ghāfir*], 'the All-Forgiving' [*al-Ghafūr*] and 'He who is full of forgiveness' [*al-Ghaffār*], it would not be improbable that these be counted as three names. For 'the Forgiver' [*al-Ghāfir*] indicates the basis of forgiveness only, while 'the All-Forgiving' [*al-Ghafūr*] indicates a multiple forgiveness in relation to many offenses—inasmuch as whoever forgives only one kind of offense is not said to be 'all-forgiving'. The 'One who is full of forgiveness', however, signifies multiplicity by way of repetition, that is, he forgives all one's offenses time and again—so that whoever forgives all one's offenses the first time, but does not forgive those who repeatedly commit offenses, would not deserve the name 'He who is full of forgiveness' [*al-Ghaffār*].

Similarly for 'the Rich' and 'the King'. 'The Rich' is one who lacks for nothing, and 'the King' is also one who lacks for nothing, while everything needs him, so 'king' communicates the meaning of 'rich' plus something more. Similarly for 'the Omniscient' [*al-ʿAlīm*] and 'He who is aware of everything' [*al-Khabīr*]: for 'omniscient' refers to knowing alone, while 'aware of everything' refers to knowing interior things, and this much dissimilarity keeps the names from being synonymous. They are in a class with 'sword' [*sayf*] and 'sword made in India' [*muhannad*] or 'sharp sword' [*ṣārim*], but not in a class with *asad* and *layth*.[12] Even if we are unable to pursue either of these two courses with some of the names close to one another in meaning, we should believe that there is a dissimilarity between the meanings of the two words. Or if we fail to specify what differentiates them, as for example, in 'immense' and 'great', where it is difficult for us to identify the point of difference between the two meanings pertaining to God most high, nevertheless we have no doubt about the principle of difference. In that respect, may he be honoured who said: 'greatness is my cloak and immensity my girdle', making a difference between them which indicates [38] dissimilarity.[13] For both cloak and girdle adorn the one who wears them, but a cloak is more elegant than a girdle.

Likewise, He made the opening phrase of prayer to be *'Allāhu akbar'*, and not even those endowed with penetrating insight would put *'Allāhu aʿẓam'* in its place. Similarly, Arabs distinguish in their use between the two words since they use *kabīr* where they do not use *ʿaẓīm*, and if they were synonymous, they would be interchangeable in every instance. Arabs say that 'so-and-so is greater in age than so-and-so', while they do not say 'more tremendous in age'. Similarly, 'the Majestic' [*al-Jalīl*] differs from 'the Great' [*al-Kabīr*] and 'the Tremendous' [*al-ʿAẓīm*], since 'majesty' refers to the attributes of eminence, and for that reason one does not say that someone is 'more majestic in age' than so-and-so; instead one says 'greater'. It is also said that 'the throne is more tremendous than a man', and not 'more majestic than a man'.[14]

So these names, although interrelated in meaning, are not synonymous. In sum, it is unlikely that the names included in the ninety-nine be synonymous since names are not intended for their letters or external differences, but rather for their meanings. This is a principle in which we should believe.

CHAPTER THREE [39]

# On one name which has different meanings and is equivocal[15] in relation to them

AN EXAMPLE of this is 'the Source of Security' [*al-Mu'min*], for what might be intended by this term is faith [*taṣdīq*], and yet it might also be derived from the word for security [*amn*] with the intent of communicating security and safety. Is it possible that it be predicated of both meanings as in the predication of a common noun to the things it names, as when 'omniscient' is predicated of knowledge of things invisible as well as visible, exterior as well as interior, and many other objects? If this be considered from a linguistic point of view, it is improbable that an equivocal term be predicated of all the things named as a common noun. For Arabs use the term 'man', intending by it every single man; that is what it is to be common. But they do not use the term 'eye' intending by it the 'eye' of the sun, of a dinar, of a scale, the spring whence water gushes forth, as well as the eye by which an animal sees. This is an equivocal term, so uses like those just mentioned intend but one of its meanings, distinguished by what is associated with it. It was told of al-Shāfiʿī—may God be pleased with him—in the *Uṣūl*, that he said: 'an equivocal term is predicated of all that it names if it appears by itself without a context to indicate the specifications'.[16] Whether this be an accurate report concerning him, it is nonetheless improbable, since the term 'eye' by itself is linguistically ambiguous unless a context indicates the specification.

So far as generalization is concerned, it is at variance with the original determination of speech. And indeed, regarding the way that revelation disposes words, it is not improbable that they be used, according to the determination and disposition of [*sharīʿa*], as one word to intend all [40] the meanings. Thus the term 'faithful' will be used, according to *sharīʿa*, for the believer and also connote security—but by the determination of *sharīʿa*, not of language. As the terms for prayer [*ṣalāt*] or fasting [*ṣiyām*] are specified by the disposition of the Law for some things which the determination of language does not impose. All this would be less conjectural were there proof for it, but there is no proof indicating that the *sharīʿa* has changed the disposition of words. In my view what is most probable is that they had not been changed, and some writers went too far when they said that if a single name from the names of God—great and glorious—can sustain many meanings such that reason does not indicate any absurdity among them, then it is to be predicated of all of them as if it were a common noun.

Certainly, there are some meanings whose closeness to each other is such as almost to resolve the differences in them to relationships, so that their ambiguity comes close to that of a common term. In such matters a polysemy is more probable, as with 'the Flawless' [*al-Salām*], where it is possible that what is intended be His flawlessness with regard to defect or shortcoming, and also possible that what is intended be the flawlessness of the creature by Him and through Him. So this term and others like it are close to common nouns. If it is determined that the more correct inclination is towards withholding specification, then seeking a determination of specific meanings will be simply a matter of individual judgment, and the arguments supporting one's judgment regarding the determination that the meanings are specific will be (1) that it is more fitting [to render *al-mu'min]* as 'what communicates security', and this is more appropriate for giving praise in regard to God—great and glorious—than 'belief', whereas the term 'belief' would be more appropriate for someone other than God, since everyone should have faith in Him and believe in His words, and the one believed-in ranks higher than the one believing. Or (2) that accepting one of these two meanings does not make two names synonymous, as may giving 'guardian' [*muhaymin*] a sense other than that of 'all-observant' [*raqīb*]. For 'guardian' [*muhaymin*] is more appropriate than 'all-observant' [*raqīb*]. We may say this because *'al-raqīb'* also appears in the list, and synonymy, as [41] we mentioned, is improbable. Or (3) one of the two meanings is more evident in customary usage and comes to people's understanding more swiftly because it is well-known; or is more demonstrative of perfection and praise. These and similar considerations should be employed in explicating the names. For each name we only mention that one meaning which we judge to be closest, and pay no attention to the rest unless we hold them to be similar, as we have mentioned. As for multiplying various remarks about the matter, we do not see any benefit in that since we do not regard equivocal terms to be common nouns.

## CHAPTER FOUR [42]

# Explaining how the perfection and happiness of man consists in conforming to the perfections of God most high, and in adorning himself with the meanings of His attributes and names insofar as this is conceivable for man

YOU should know that whoever has no part in the meanings of the names of God—great and glorious—except that he hear the words and understand the linguistic meaning of their explication and their determination, and except that he believe with his heart in the reality of their meanings in God most high—such a one has an ill-fated lot and a lowly rank, and ought not boast of what he has achieved. For hearing the words requires only the soundness of the sense of hearing, through which sounds are perceived, and this is a level in which beasts share. As for understanding their determination in language, all one needs is a knowledge of Arabic and this level is shared by those adept in language and even by those Bedouin who are ignorant of it.[17] As for faith affirming their meanings of God—may He be praised and exalted—without any revelatory vision,[18] all one needs is to understand the meaning of the words and to have faith in them, and this level is shared by the common people, even by young boys. For once one has understood the teaching, if these meanings were presented to him, he would [i] receive them and memorize them, [ii] believe them in his heart and [iii] persist in them. These are the levels of most scholars, to say nothing of those who are not scholars. In relation to those who do not share with them in those three levels, these should not be denied credit, yet they are clearly deficient with respect to the acme of perfection. For 'the merits of the [merely] pious are demerits in those who have drawn near to God'. Indeed those who have drawn near to Him share in the meanings of the names of God the most high in a threefold way. [43]

The first share is a knowledge of these meanings by way of witnessing and unveiling,[19] so that their essential realities are clarified for them by a proof which does not permit any error; and God's possession of these meanings as His characteristics is revealed to them in a disclosure equivalent in clarity to the certainty achieved by a man in regard to his own inner qualities, which he perceives by seeing his inward aspect, not by outward sensation. How great a difference there is between this and a faith derived from one's parents and teachers by conformity and persistence in it, even though it be accompanied by argumentative proofs from *Kalām!*[20]

A second way of sharing in these meanings belongs to those who so highly esteem what is disclosed to them of the attributes of majesty that their high regard releases a longing to possess this attribute in every way possible to them, so that they may grow closer to the Truth—in quality not in place; and with the possession of such characteristics they become similar to the angels, who have been brought near to God—great and glorious. Moreover, it is inconceivable that a heart be filled with high regard for such an attribute and be illuminated by it without a longing for this attribute following upon it, as well as a passionate love[21] for that perfection and majesty, intent upon being adorned with that attribute in its totality—inasmuch as that is possible to one who so esteems it. And if not in its totality, the esteem for this attribute will necessarily provoke in him the longing for as much of it as he can assimilate.

No-one will lack this longing except for one of two reasons: either from inadequate knowledge and certainty that the attribute in question is one of the attributes of majesty and perfection, or from the fact that one's heart is filled with another longing and absorbed by it. For when a disciple observes the perfection of his master in knowledge, longing will be triggered in him to be like him and to follow his example—unless he be filled with hunger, for example, so that the preoccupation of his innards for food could prevent the longing for knowledge from arising in him. [44] So it is necessary for the one who would contemplate the attributes of God most high to have emptied his heart of desiring anything except God—great and glorious. For knowledge is the seed of longing, but only to the extent that it encounters a heart freed from the thorns of the passions, for unless the heart be empty the seed will not bear fruit.

The third share follows upon the effort to acquire whatever is possible of those attributes, to imitate them and be adorned with their good qualities, for in this way man becomes 'lordly'—that is, close to the Lord most high, and so becomes a companion to the heavenly host [*al-mala' al-aʿlā*] of angels, for they are on the carpet of proximity [to God].[22] Indeed, whoever aims at a likeness to their qualities will attain something of their closeness to the extent that he acquires some of their attributes which bring them closer to the Truth most high.

Now you may say: seeking closeness to God—great and glorious—by way of attributes is so obscure a proposal that hearts are at the point of recoiling from accepting it or from believing in it; so you should develop an explanation to defuse the vehemence of those who reject it, for to the majority this will be considered to be forbidden unless its truth be disclosed. To which I say: it is not a secret to you, nor to a scholar who has developed even a little above the level of the common scholar, that existing things are divided into perfect and imperfect, and that the perfect are nobler than the imperfect, and that no matter how different the degrees of perfection may be, ultimate perfection is limited to One—so that no one is simply perfect but He. Other existing things do not have perfection simply, but different perfections belong to them in relation [to Him]; for there is no doubt that a thing is more perfect the closer it is to He Who has perfection simply—closer, that is, in degree and in level, not in perfection *tout court.*

Existing things are divided into animate and inanimate, and you know that living things are nobler and more perfect than the non-living, and that there are three levels of living things: the level of angels, the level of man, [45] and the level of beasts. Beasts rank at the bottom in that very life which distinguishes them, for life lies in perception and in activity, yet beasts are imperfect in perception and in action. The deficiency in their perception lies in its being limited to the senses, and sensory perception is limited because it only perceives things by contact or proximity. Without contact or proximity, a sense faculty is cut off from perception. For taste and touch require contact, while hearing, sight and smell need proximity. The senses are instantly cut off from perceiving any existing thing which cannot be conceived to be in contact or proximity to them. Furthermore, their activity is limited to what is dictated by passion or anger, and cannot be triggered by anything else, for they lack reason to summon them to activities which differ from the demands of passion and anger.

As for angels, theirs is the highest level because they are existents whose perception is not affected by proximity or distance. Nor is their perception limited to what is conceivable as close by or far away, since proximity and distance are conceived for bodies, and bodies are the lowest of the categories of existing things. Furthermore, angels are too holy for passion and anger, so their activity is not dictated by passion or anger; rather what moves them to engage in activity is something more exalted than passion and anger, namely, to seek proximity to God the most high.

So far as man is concerned, his level is midway between the other two, as though he were composed of bestial and angelic natures. At the beginning of his life, his bestial nature predominates, since the only perception he has at first is through the senses, perception which requires that he seek [46] proximity to the thing sensed through pursuit and movement. Eventually the light of reason dawns upon him, which disposes itself through the realms of heaven and earth, with no need for bodily motion nor for seeking proximity or contact with what it perceives. Rather, its objects of perception are exempt from proximity or distance in space. Similarly, passion and anger hold sway over him at first, and desires arise in accordance with what they dictate, until the desire to seek perfection appears in him, and he considers consequences and begins to resist the demands of passion and anger. If he conquers passion and anger to the point of controlling them, and they become too weak to move him or pacify him, he then attains a likeness to the angels. Likewise, if he weans himself from the inflexibility of things imagined and perceptible through the senses, and accustoms himself to perceiving things too exalted to be attained by sense or imagination, he will achieve another likeness to the angels. For the specific properties of living things are perception and activity, and both of them are susceptible to deficiency, moderate status, or perfection. The more one emulates the angels in these specific properties, the more is one removed from one's bestial nature and comes close to the angelic. For the angels are close to God—great and glorious—and whoever is close to one who is close is himself close.

You may say: this teaching apparently points to affirming a likeness between man and God most high, because one who conforms himself to His perfections is made to be like Him, whereas it is known by revelation and by reason concerning God—may He be praised and exalted—*that naught is as His likeness* (XLII:11): that He does not resemble anything nor does anything resemble Him. Then I say: the more you know the meaning of the likeness denied of God—great and glorious—the more you will know that there is no likeness of Him, nor should one think that sharing in every attribute requires that there be a likeness. [47]

When two contraries are so remote from each other that one cannot conceive of yet more distance between them, would you consider them to be like one another simply because they share in many attributes—as blackness shares with whiteness being an accident, a colour, perceived by sight, and other similar features? Would you consider that one who says that God—great and glorious—exists but not in a subject, that He enjoys hearing, seeing, knowing, willing, speaking, living, power, acting, and that man is also like that, thereby likens God to creatures and affirms a likeness? Not at all! That is not the way it is, for if it were, then every creature would bear a likeness to Him, since the least one can do is affirm a share in existence, and that instills the illusion of likeness. But a likeness is defined as sharing in a specific kind and a quiddity. For even if a horse is extremely adroit, it still bears no likeness to a man, because they are of different species—it is only like a man in adroitness, which is an accident outside the quiddity constituting the essence of humanity.

The specifying mark of divinity is that God is an existent necessarily existing in Himself, such that everything whose existence is possible exists from Him [if it does exist], according to the best ways of order and perfection.[23] It is inconceivable that this specifying mark be shared in at all, or that anything attain a likeness to it. If man's being merciful, patient, or grateful does not require the existence of a likeness, neither will his hearing, seeing, knowing, power, living, or acting. Rather, I hold that the specifying mark of divinity belongs to none but God—the most high and to be held holy—and no one knows it but God, nor is it conceivable that anyone know it except Him or one like Him. And since there is no likeness of Him, He or 'His nature' is not known by other than Him. So al-Junayd—may God's mercy be upon him—was right when he remarked: 'Only

God knows God'.[24] For that reason He only gave His noblest [48] creature [Muḥammad] a name which veiled Himself, as He said: *Praise the name of thy Lord most high* (LXXXVII:1). So, by God, no one other than God knows God, in this world or the next.

Dhu'l-Nūn was asked, when he was on the brink of death: 'What do you long for?' and he said: 'that I might see Him before I die—be it only for an instant'.[25] Now this confuses the hearts of most of the weak and induces them to accept the teaching of negation and denial of all attributes to God, and this may be attributed to their inability to understand this discussion.[26]

For I say: if one were to say: 'I know only God', he would be right, and if he said: 'I do not know God', he would be correct. Yet we know that negation and affirmation cannot be true at once, but that truth must be distinguished from falsity so that if a negation be true the affirmation is false, and vice-versa. But in different respects it is conceivable that things said on both sides be true. This would be the case were one person to say to another: 'do you know the faithful one Abū Bakr—may God be pleased with him?',[27] and he were to say: 'Is the faithful one [*as-ṣiddīq*] unheard of or not known? Given the fame, visibility and renown of his name, is it conceivable that anyone in the world not know him? Is there anything but his name on the pulpits? Is there anything other than his mention in the mosques? Is there anything other than his praise and description on people's tongues?' So the one who says this would be right. But if another were asked: 'do you know him?' and he said: 'Who am I to know the faithful one? Far from it! Only one who is faithful knows the faithful one, or someone who is like him or above him. Who am I to claim to know him or even hope for that? People like me hear his name and his attributes, [49] but as for claiming to know him—that would be impossible'. This statement would also be right—indeed it comes closer to the glorification and esteem [due to Abū Bakr].

This is the way in which one should understand the one who says 'I know God' and the one who says 'I do not know God'.

If you were to show a piece of intelligible writing to a reasonable person and say to him: 'do you know its writer?' and he said 'no', he would be speaking truly. But if he said 'yes: its writer is a man living and powerful, hearing and seeing, sound of hand and knowledgeable in the practise of writing, and if I know all this from [the sample] how can I not know him?—he too would be speaking truly. Yet the saying of the one who said 'I do not know him' is more correct and true, for in reality he has not known him. Rather he only knows that intelligible writing requires a living writer, knowing, powerful, hearing, and seeing; yet he does not know the writer himself. Similarly, every creature knows only that this ordered and precisely disposed world requires an arranging, living, knowing, and powerful maker.

This knowledge has two dimensions: one of them concerns the world; and has for its object the need that someone direct it; while the other pertains to God—great and glorious—and has for its object names derived from attributes, which do not enter into the reality of the essence and its quiddity. We have already explained that when one points to something and says: 'what is it?' to mention names derived from it is no answer at all. For if he pointed to an individual animal and said: 'what is it?' and the response was tall or white or short; or if he pointed to water and said: 'what is it?' and the response was: it is cold; or [50] to fire, asking: 'what is it?' and the response was hot—none of that would answer concerning the quiddity at all. Knowing something is to know its essential reality and its quiddity, not the names derived from it. For our saying 'hot' means something or other with the attribute of heat, similarly our saying 'powerful' or 'knowing' means something or other with the attribute of power or knowledge.

If you say: our saying that He is the necessary existent from whom alone exists every single thing whose existence is possible, is equivalent to His essential reality and His definition, and we already know that; I would say: not at all! For our saying 'necessary existent' is equivalent to His having no need for a cause or an agent, and this proceeds from the negation of any cause in this regard. And our saying 'every existing thing exists from Him' proceeds from actions being related to Him. So if we are asked: what is this thing? and we answer: He is an agent; that would not be an answer. Or if we said: He is the one who has a cause, that would not be an answer either, so how must it be with our statement: He is the one who has no cause? For all such discourse discloses what is not His essence or what relates to His essence either by negation or affirmation, and so entirely comprises names, attributes, or relations.

If you say: what is the way to knowing Him? I would say: were a small boy or an impotent person to say to us: what is the way to know the pleasure of sexual intercourse, and to perceive its essential reality? we would say: there are two ways here: one of them is for us to describe it to you, so that you can know it; the other is to wait patiently until you experience the natural instinct of passion in yourself, and then for you to engage in intercourse so that you experience the pleasure of intercourse yourself, and so come to know it. This second way is the authentic way, leading to the reality of knowledge.

The first way leads only to an imagining and to comparing it with something which is not like it, since the most we can do is represent the pleasure of intercourse by something whose pleasures an impotent person can experience, like the pleasure of food and refreshing drink. So we would say to him: 'Do you not know that sweets are delicious, [51] for when you take some, you reach a pleasant state and feel delight in your soul?' He will say 'certainly' and then we would say: 'sexual intercourse is like that as well'. Do you think that this brings him to understand the real pleasure of intercourse as it is, to the point of occupying in his knowledge the place occupied in one who has tasted that pleasure and experienced it? Hardly! In fact, the most that this description could be would be an imagining and a misleading comparison, an illustration sharing nothing but the name.

So far as the imagining is concerned, he would imagine that it [intercourse] was something pleasant in a general way. As for the comparison, it amounts to likening intercourse to the sweetness of sugar, and this is misleading since there is no correspondence whatever between the sweetness of sugar and the pleasure of intercourse. And as far as sharing in the name is concerned, he knows that it deserves to be called pleasure; yet when the passion arises and he experiences it, he will know that the sweetness of sugar is not like it at all, and what he had imagined of it was not at all what he imagined. Indeed, he will know that whatever he had heard about its name and attributes—that it was pleasurable and good—was true, but far more true of the passion of intercourse than of the sweetness of sugar.

Similarly, there are two ways of knowing God—may He be praised and exalted: one of them inadequate and the other closed. The inadequate way consists in mentioning names and attributes and proceeding to compare them with what we know from ourselves. For when we know ourselves to be powerful, knowing, living, speaking, and then hear those terms attributed to God—great and glorious, or when we come to know them by demonstration, in either case we understand them with an inadequate comprehension, much as the impotent person understood the pleasure of intercourse from what was described for him of the pleasure of sweets. Indeed, our life, power, and understanding are farther from the life,- power, and understanding of God—great and glorious—than sugar's sweetness is from the pleasure of intercourse. In fact, there is no correspondence between them. The outcome of defining God—great and glorious—by these attributes, then, is but establishing imaginings and likenesses, and a sharing in the name. But the process of comparison is cut short when it is said: *Naught is as His likeness* (XLII:11), for He is living but not like living things, [52] powerful but not like powerful persons, much as you would say: intercourse is pleasurable like sweets, but sexual pleasure is totally unlike that of sweets, although they do share in the name.

This amounts to saying that when we know God most high to be living, powerful and knowing, we are only knowing ourselves, as we only know Him by way of ourselves. For the deaf cannot conceivably understand the meaning of our saying that God hears, nor can the blind understand the meaning of our saying that He sees. Therefore, when one asks how God—great and glorious—might be said to know things, we answer: just as you know things. And if one asks: how might He be powerful, we answer: as you are powerful. For a man cannot understand anything unless he has in him something corresponding to it. He first knows what characterizes him, and then knows something other than himself by analogy with it. So if God had an attribute or a specifying property, and there were nothing in us corresponding to it or sharing its name—even so much as the sweetness of sugar shares in the pleasure of intercourse—it would be inconceivable that we would ever understand [that attribute or property] at all. For each person only understands himself, and then compares his own attributes with those of God the most high. Yet His attributes are too exalted to be likened to ours! So this will be an inadequate knowledge in which imagining and resemblances are preponderant. So it needs to be complemented by the knowledge which denies any likeness, and which rejects any grounds for commensurability, even though the name be shared.

The second way—the one that is closed—consists in one's waiting to attain all the 'lordly' [i.e., divine] attributes to the point of becoming a 'lord', much as a boy waits until he matures [53] to experience the pleasure of intercourse. But this path is closed, since it is impossible that this reality be attained by anyone other than God the most high. There is no other way to authentic knowledge than this, yet it is utterly closed except for God the most high and holy One.

Therefore, it is impossible for anyone other than God truly to know God most high. But I would also say: it is impossible for anyone other than a prophet to know a prophet. For whoever has no part in prophecy understands nothing of prophethood except the name: that it is a property existing in a man which distinguishes him from one who is not a prophet; yet he does not know the quiddity of that property except by comparison with his own attributes.

But I would go even further and say: no-one knows the essential reality of death or of paradise or of hell until after death when one enters into paradise or hell. For paradise is equivalent to a source of pleasure, and if we were to posit a person who had never experienced any pleasure, it would be utterly impossible for us to make him understand paradise with an understanding which would awaken in him a desire to seek it. Hell is equivalent to a source of suffering, and if we were to posit a person who had never suffered pain, it would not be possible for us to make such a person understand hell. But if he has suffered it, we can make him understand it by comparing it to the worst pain he has ever suffered, namely the pain of fire.

By the same token, if someone has experienced any pleasure, all we can do to make him understand paradise is to compare it with the greatest pleasures ever granted him—from food, sexual intercourse, or feasting his eyes on beauty. If there be pleasures in paradise different from these pleasures, there is no way at all to make him understand them except by comparison with these pleasures, as we remarked in comparing the pleasures of intercourse with the sweetness of sugar. Yet the pleasures of paradise are still farther from all the pleasures we experience in this world than are the pleasures of intercourse from the pleasure of sweets. Indeed the apt expression of them has it that 'they are what no eye has seen nor ear heard, [54] nor have they occurred to the heart of man'.[28] For if we compared these pleasures with food, we should say: not like this food; and if we compared them with intercourse, we should say: not like the intercourse we are familiar with in this life. Why would others be surprised at our saying: what the people of earth and of heaven attain of God most high is only His attributes and names, when we say that what they attain of heaven is only its attributes and the names? The same is true for everything whose name and attribute man has heard though he has never experienced or perceived the thing itself, nor may he be said to have attained it or be characterized by it.

If you say: what is the ultimate point of knowledge attained by the 'knowers' of God the most high? We would say: the ultimate knowledge of the 'knowers' lies in their inability to know, in their realizing in fact that they do not know Him and that it is utterly impossible for them to know Him; indeed, that it is impossible for anyone except God to know God with an authentic knowledge comprehending the true nature of the divine attributes.[29] If that is disclosed to them by proof, as we have mentioned, they will know it—that is, they will have attained the utmost to which creatures can possibly attain in knowing Him.

This is what the most faithful one [*al-ṣiddīq*] Abū Bakr (may God be pleased with him) pointed out when he said: 'the failure to attain perception is itself a perception'. And this is what the master of men [the Prophet]—may God's blessing and peace be upon him—meant when he said: 'I cannot enumerate Your praise; You are as You have praised Yourself'.[30] He did not mean by this that he knew of Him what his tongue was unable to express about Him, but he rather meant: 'I do not comprehend Your praises and divine attributes; You alone are the one to comprehend them'. Therefore no created thing can enjoy the authentic vision of His essence except in bewilderment and confusion. So the scope of knowledge consists in knowledge of the names and the attributes. [55]

You may ask: since it is inconceivable to know Him, how can the ranks of angels, prophets, and holy men be said to differ in knowing Him? I would respond: you already know that there are two ways of knowing; one of them is the authentic way which is in fact closed to all but God the most high. Every creature who is moved to attain and perceive Him will be cast back by the splendour of His majesty, nor is there anyone who cranes his neck to see Him whose glance is not turned aside in amazement.

The second way—knowledge of attributes and names—is open to creatures and their ranking in it differs. For whoever (1) knows that He—great and glorious—is knowing and powerful, but in a general fashion, is not like one who (2) witnesses the wonders of His signs in the realm of the heavens and the earth, and the creating of spirits and bodies, and examines the wonders of the kingdom and the prodigies of workmanship; closely scrutinizing the details, inquiring into the fine points of wisdom, acknowledging in full the subtleties of organization, and is so characterized by all of the angelic attributes which bring them close to God—great and glorious—that by attaining these properties he is in fact characterized by them. Between these two modes of knowing lies an immense distance which it is not possible to measure, while prophets and holy men differ in these details and in their capacities.

You will come to understand this only by an example, and *Allah's is the sublime similitude* (XVI:60). You know that a pious and perfect scholar like al-Shāfiʿī, for example—may God be pleased with him—is known by the porter of his house as well as by al-Muzanī, his disciple—may God have mercy on him.[31] The porter knows in a general fashion that he is learned in the law and has written on it, and has guided the people of God—great and glorious—to it. Al-Muzanī knows him, however, not like the porter, but with a knowledge encompassing in detail his qualities and what he knows. But a scholar who is proficient in ten branches of knowledge is not really known by a disciple of his [56] who has learned only one field, to say nothing of his servant who has learned nothing of his knowledge. Indeed, whoever has acquired one field of knowledge in fact knows but one-tenth of his master, provided he so equals him in that science that he does not fall short of him. For if he falls short of him, then he does not really know what he falls short of, except by name and an imagination of its entirety; yet he does know that his master knows something different than what he knows. Similarly, you should understand that creatures differ in knowledge of God the most high in proportion to what is revealed to them from the things known of God—great and glorious: the marvels of His power and the wonders of His signs in this world and the next, and in the visible and invisible world. In this way their knowledge of God—great and glorious—is enhanced, and their knowledge comes close to that of God most High.[32]

Now you might ask: but if they do not really know the essence of God and if knowledge of it is impossible, do they then know the names and qualities with a perfect and authentic knowledge? We would say: not at all! Not even that is known perfectly and authentically except by God—great and glorious. For if we knew that a being were a knower, we would know something about it, without being aware of its essential reality but realizing that it has the attribute of knowledge. And if we knew the attribute of knowledge in its essential reality, our knowledge that it is a knower would be a perfect knowledge of the essential reality of this attribute—otherwise it would not be. Yet no one knows the essential reality of God's knowledge—great and glorious—without having a likeness of His knowledge. But only God has that, since no-one other than Him knows it. Others know it only by comparing it with their own knowledge, as we showed in the example comparing such knowledge to that of sweets. But the knowledge of God—great and glorious—is totally unlike the knowledge of creatures, so the knowledge creatures have of Him will neither be perfect nor authentic, but illusory and anthropomorphic.

You should not be surprised at this, for I would also say: no one knows the sorcerer but the sorcerer himself [57] or a sorcerer like him or superior to him. Whoever does not know sorcery in its essential reality and its quiddity knows the name 'sorcerer' and that he has knowledge and a special quality, yet he does not realize what that knowledge is, for he does not know the things the sorcerer knows nor does he perceive what that special quality is. Indeed, he does realize that the special quality, obscure as it may be, is a specific kind of knowledge whose result is to change hearts and alter the attributes of individuals, as well as to enjoy clairvoyance and set married couples at odds with each other; yet this remains far from an authentic knowledge of sorcery. And whoever does not know the essential reality of sorcery does not know what a sorcerer is either, since a sorcerer is one with the special property of sorcery, and the content of the name 'sorcerer' is a term derived from an attribute; so if that attribute is unknown the sorcerer will not be known either, yet he will be known if the attribute is. What is known of sorcery to one who is not a sorcerer is but a generic description far from the quiddity: that it is a specific kind of knowledge, and that the term knowledge is applied to it.

Similarly, the content, in our view, of the power of God—great and glorious—is that of an attribute whose effect and trace is the existence of things, and the term 'power' is applied to it because it corresponds to our power much as the pleasure of intercourse corresponds to the pleasure of sweets. All of this is quite apart from the essential reality of that power. Indeed, the more a man comprehends of the details of the things which have been decreed, and the workmanship in the kingdom of the heavens, the more abundant his share will be in knowing the attribute of power. For by their fruits the fruitful are known; in the way that the more a pupil comprehends the details of his master's learning, and his writings, the more perfect is his knowledge of him, and the more complete his esteem for him.

Now the difference in the knowledge of the 'knowers' comes to this, and it is possessed by an unending difference, because there is no limit to what a man cannot attain regarding what may be known of God the most high, nor is there a limit to what he is able to know, even though what is included in his actual knowledge is limited. [58] Yet the human potential for knowledge is unlimited. Indeed what comes into existence differs in abundance and rarity, and so the differences are evident—like the disparity in power among men which comes to them from wealth in property. One may own one-sixth of a dirham or a dirham, while another owns thousands. The case is similar with forms of knowing, although the disparity among forms of knowing is even greater because the range of things to be known has no limits, whereas material goods are bodies and it can hardly be denied that bodies are limited in number.

Now you have come to know how creatures differ in the sea of knowing God—great and glorious—and that their difference is without limit. You have also known that one may rightly say: 'No one other than God knows God', and that one may also rightly say: 'I know only God'. For there is nothing in existence except God—great and glorious—and His works. And if one were to consider His works insofar as they are His works, and the consideration were so focussed on this that he did not see them in as much as they be sky or earth or trees, but in so far as He made them, then his knowledge would not embrace anything other than the divine presence, so that it would be possible for him to say: 'I know only God and I see only God—great and glorious'.

Were it conceivable that a person see only the sun and its light spreading over the horizon, it would be right for him to say: I see only the sun, for the light radiating from it is part of the whole and not extrinsic to it. So everything in existence is a light from the lights of the eternal power, and a trace from its traces.[33] And as the sun is the source of light radiating to every illuminated thing, so in a similar fashion the meaning which words fall short of expressing—though it was necessarily expressed as 'the eternal power'—is the source of existence radiating to every existing thing. [59] Yet there is nothing in existence but God—great and glorious—so it is possible for a knower to say: 'I know only God'.[34]

It is odd that one may say: 'I know only God', and be right, and say: 'Only God—great and glorious—knows God', yet also be right. But each reflects a particular intention. If mutually contradictory statements were untruthful when respects of consideration differ, the saying of the most high would not be accurate: *You did not throw when you threw, but God threw* (VIII:17).[35] Yet it is accurate, since there are two interpretations of throwing: on one it is attributed to man, while on the second to the Lord most high—and in this way the statement is not contradictory.

Let us pull back the reins of discourse right here, for we have plunged into the depth of a shoreless sea, and secrets like these ought not be abused by putting them down in books; and since this was not intended but has happened by accident, let us refrain from it, and return to explaining in detail the meanings of the beautiful names of God.

## PART TWO

### CHAPTER ONE [63]

# On Explaining the Meanings of God's Ninety-Nine Names

THESE are the names comprised in the account of Abū Hurayra—may God be pleased with him—when he said: 'The Messenger of God—may God's blessing and peace be upon him—said: God—great and glorious—has ninety-nine names, one hundred minus one; single, He loves odd numbers, and whoever enumerates them will enter Paradise'.[1]

He is (1) *Allāh* and there is no other god but He: (2) *Al-Raḥmān* (The Infinitely Good), (3) *Al-Raḥīm* (The Merciful), (4) *Al-Malik* (The King), (5) *Al-Quddūs* (The Holy), (6) *Al-Salām* (The Flawless), (7) *Al-Mu'min* (The Faithful), (8) *Al-Muhaymin* (The Guardian), (9) *Al-ʿAzīz* (The Eminent), (10) *Al-Jabbār* (The Compeller), (11) *Al-Mutakabbir* (The Proud), (12) *Al-Khāliq* (The Creator), (13) *Al-Bāri'* (The Producer), (14) *Al-Muṣawwir* (The Fashioner), (15) *Al-Ghaffār* (He who is full of forgiveness), (16) *Al-Qahhār* (The Dominator), (17) *Al-Wahhāb* (The Bestower), (18) *Al-Razzāq* (The Provider), (19) *Al-Fattāḥ* (The Opener), (20) *Al-ʿAlīm* (The Omniscient), (21) *Al-Qābiḍ* (He who contracts), (22) *Al-Bāsiṭ* (He who expands), (23) *Al-Khāfiḍ* (The Abaser), (24) *Al-Rāfiʿ* (The Exalter), (25) *Al-Muʿizz* (The Honourer), (26) *Al-Mudhill* (He who humbles), (27) *Al-Samīʿ* (The All-Hearing), (28) *Al-Baṣīr* (The All-Seeing), (29) *Al-Ḥakam* (The Arbitrator), (30) *Al-ʿAdl* (The Just), (31) *Al-Laṭīf* (The Benevolent), (32) *Al-Khabīr* (The Totally Aware), (33)

*Al-Ḥalīm* (The Mild), (34) *Al-ʿAẓīm* (The Tremendous), (35) *Al-Ghafūr* (The All-Forgiving), (36) *Al-Shakūr* (The Grateful), (37) *Al-ʿAlī* (The Most High), (38) *Al-Kabīr* (The Great), (39) *Al-Ḥafīẓ* (The All-Preserver), (40) *Al-Muqīt* (The Nourisher), (41) *Al-Ḥasīb* (The Reckoner), (42) *Al-Jalīl* (The Majestic), (43) *Al-Karīm* (The Generous), (44) *Al-Raqīb* (The All-Observant), (45) *Al-Mujīb* (The Answerer of prayers), (46) *Al-Wāsiʿ* (The Vast), (47) *Al-Ḥakīm* (The Wise), (48) *Al-Wadūd* (The Lovingkind), (49) *Al-Majīd* (The All-Glorious), (50) *Al-Bāʿith* (The Raiser of the dead), (51) *Al-Shahīd* (The Universal Witness), (52) *Al-Ḥaqq* (The Truth), (53) *Al-Wakīl* (The Guardian), (54) *Al-Qawī* (The Strong), (55) *Al-Matīn* (The Firm), (56) *Al-Walī* (The Patron), (57) *Al-Ḥamīd* (The Praised), (58) *Al-Muḥṣī* (The Knower of each separate thing), (59) *Al-Mubdiʿ* (The Beginner, The Cause), (60) *Al-Muʿīd* (The Restorer), (61) *Al-Muḥyī* (The Life-Giver), (62) *Al-Mumīt* (The Slayer), (63) *Al-Ḥayy* (The Living), (64) *Al-Qayyūm* (The Self-Existing), (65) *Al-Wājid* (The Resourceful), (66) *Al-Mājid* (The Magnificent), (67) *Al-Wāḥid* (The Unique), (68) *Al-Ṣamad* (The Eternal), (69) *Al-Qādir* (The All-Powerful), (70) *Al-Muqtadir* (The All-Determiner), (71) *Al-Muqaddim* (The Promoter), (72) *Al-Mu'akhkhir* (The Postponer), (73) *Al-Awwal* (The First), (74) *Al-Ākhir* (The Last), (75) *Al-Ẓāhir* (The Manifest), (76) *Al-Bāṭin* (The Hidden), (77) *Al-Wālī* (The Ruler), (78) *Al-Mutaʿālī* (The Exalted), (79) *Al-Barr* (The Doer of Good), (80) *At-Tawwāb* (The Ever-relenting), (81) *Al-Muntaqim* (The Avenger), (82) *Al-ʿAfū* (The Effacer of sins), (83) *Al-Ra'ūf* (The All-Pitying), (84) *Mālik al-Mulk* (The King of Absolute Sovereignty), (85) *Dhū' l-Jalāl wa 'l-Ikrām* (The Lord of Majesty and Generosity), (86) *Al-Muqsiṭ* (The Equitable),[2] (87) *Al-Jāmiʿ* (The Uniter), (88) *Al-Ghanī* (The Rich), (89) *Al-Mughnī* (The Enricher), (90) *Al-Māniʿ* (The Protector), (91) *Al-Ḍārr* (The Punisher), (92) *Al-Nāfiʿ* (He who benefits), (93) *Al-Nūr* (Light), (94) *Al-Hādī* (The Guide), (95) *Al-Badīʿ* (The Absolute Cause), (96) *Al-Bāqī* (The Everlasting), (97) *Al-Wārith*

(The Inheritor), (98) *Al-Rashīd* (The Right in Guidance), (99) *Al-Ṣabūr* (The Patient). [64]

As for His saying *Allāh*, it is a name for the true existent, the one who unites the attributes of divinity, is subject of the attributes of lordship, and unique in true existence. For no existent thing other than He may claim to exist of itself, but rather it gains existence from Him: it is perishing insofar as it exists of itself, and exists insofar as it faces Him. For every existing thing *is perishing except His face.*[3] It is most likely that in indicating *this* meaning [*Allāh*] is analogous to proper names, so everything which has been said about its derivation and definition is arbitrary and artificial.

*A lesson.* You should know that this name is the greatest of the ninety-nine names of God—great and glorious—because it refers to the essence which unites all the attributes of divinity, so that none of them is left out, whereas each of the remaining names only refers to a single attribute: knowledge, power, agency, and the rest. It is also the most specific of the names, since no-one uses it for anyone other than Him, neither literally nor metaphorically, whereas the rest of the names may name things other than He, as in 'the Powerful', 'the Knowing', 'the Merciful', and the rest. So in these two respects it seems that this name is the greatest of these names.

*Implications.* It is conceivable that man appropriate something of the meanings of the rest of the names, to the point that the name be used of him—as in 'the Merciful', 'the Knowing', 'the Indulgent', 'the Patient', 'the Grateful', and the rest; although the name is used of him in a way quite different from its use for God—great and glorious. Yet the meaning of this name, *Allāh*, is so specific that it is inconceivable that it be shared, either metaphorically or literally. On account of this specificity the rest of the names are described as names *of*

God—great and glorious—and are defined in relation to Him: it is said that 'the Patient', 'the Grateful', 'the King', and 'the Restorer' are among the names of God—great and glorious, but it is not said that *'Allāh'* is among the names of the grateful [One] and the patient [One]. That is because *'Allāh'* [i.e., 'God'], to the extent that it is more indicative of the very being of the meanings of divinity and consequently more specific, [65] is better known and more evident, so that it does not need to be defined by something other than it, but rather the others are defined by relation to it.

*Counsel*: Man's share in this name should be for him to become god-like [*ta'alluh*], by which I mean that his heart and his aspiration be taken up with God—great and glorious, that he not look towards anything other than Him nor pay attention to what is not He, that he neither implore nor fear anyone but Him.[4] How could it be otherwise? For it had already been understood from this name that He is the truly actual Existent, and that everything other than He is ephemeral, perishing and worthless except in relation to Him. [The servant] sees himself first of all as the first of the perishing and worthless, as did the messenger of God—may God's grace and peace be upon him—when he said: 'the truest verse uttered by the Arabs was Labīd's saying:

> Surely everything except God is vain,
> And every happiness is doubtless ephemeral.[5]

2, 3. *Al-Raḥmān, Al-Raḥīm*—The Infinitely Good, the Merciful—are two names derived from 'mercy'. Mercy requires an object of mercy, and no one is an object of mercy unless he be in need. Yet the one by whom the needs of the needy are fulfilled will not be called merciful if that is accomplished without intention, volition, or concern for the one in need. Nor is one called merciful who wants to fulfil their needs yet does not meet them even though he be able to fulfil them, because if the will were there he would have carried it out. But if he be unable to fulfil them, he is still called merciful—though in a deficient sense—in view of the empathy which affected him. Perfect mercy is pouring out benefaction to those in need, and directing it to them, for their care; and inclusive mercy is when it embraces deserving and undeserving alike. The mercy of God—great and glorious—is both perfect and inclusive [*tāmma wa-ʿāmma*]: perfect inasmuch as it wants to fulfil the needs of those in need and does meet them; and inclusive inasmuch as it embraces both deserving and undeserving, encompassing this world and the next, and includes bare necessities and needs, and special gifts over and above them. So He is utterly and truly merciful. [66]

*Implications.* Mercy is not without a painful empathy which affects the merciful, and moves him to satisfy the needs of the one receiving mercy. Yet the Lord—praise be to Him most high—transcends that, so you may think that this diminishes the meaning of mercy. But you should know that this is a perfection and does not diminish the meaning of mercy. It is not diminished inasmuch as the perfection of mercy depends on the perfection of its fruits. So long as the needs of those in need are perfectly fulfilled, the one who receives mercy has no need of suffering or distress in the merciful one; rather the suffering of the merciful only stems from a weakness and defect in himself. Moreover, this weakness adds nothing to the goal of those in need once their needs have been perfectly fulfilled. So far as God's mercy perfectly fulfilling the meaning of mercy is concerned, we should recall that one who is merciful out of empathy and suffering comes close to intending to alleviate his own suffering and sensitivity by his actions, thereby looking after himself and seeking his own goals, and that would take away from the perfection of the meaning of mercy.[6] Rather, the perfection of mercy consists in looking after the one receiving mercy for the sake of the one receiving mercy, and not for the sake of being relieved from one's own suffering and sensitivity.

*Lesson. Al-Raḥmān* is more specific than *Al-Raḥīm*, in that no one except God—great and glorious—is named by it, whereas *Al-Raḥīm* may be used for others. In this respect [*Al-Raḥmān*] is close to the name of God most high which functions like a proper name [*Allāh*], although it is definitely derived from mercy [*raḥma*]. To that end God—great and glorious—has combined them both in saying: *Call upon God or call upon the Infinitely Good; whichever you call upon, to Him belong the names most beautiful* (XVII:110). In this respect, given our ruling out synonymy among the enumerated names, we should distinguish between the meanings of the two names. More precisely, the meaning of *Raḥmān* should be a kind of mercy beyond the powers of people, and related to happiness in the next life. The Infinitely Good is He who loves [67] men, first by creating them; second, by guiding them to faith and to the means of salvation; third, by making them happy in the next world; and fourth, by granting them the contemplation of His noble face.[7]

*Counsel*: Man's share in the name *al-Raḥmān* lies in his showing mercy to the negligent, dissuading them from the path of negligence towards God—great and glorious—by exhortation and counselling, by way of gentleness not violence, regarding the disobedient with eyes of mercy and not contempt; letting every insubordination perpetrated in the world be as his own misfortune, so sparing no effort to eliminate it to the extent that he can—all out of mercy to the disobedient lest they be exposed to God's wrath and so deserve to be removed from proximity to Him.

His share in the name *al-Raḥīm* lies in not turning away from any needy persons without meeting their needs to the extent of his ability, nor turning from any poor in his neighbourhood or town without committing himself to them and ridding them of their poverty—either from his own wealth or reputation, or by interceding on their behalf with another. And if he be unable to do all that, he should assist them by prayer or by showing grief on account of their need, in sympathy and love towards them, as though he were thereby sharing in their misfortune and their need.

*A question and its answer.* You might say: what does it mean for Him, the most high, to be merciful and to be the most merciful of those who are merciful? For one who is merciful does not see people afflicted or injured, tormented or sick, without hastening to remove that condition when he can do so. But the Lord—praise be to Him most high—has the power to meet every affliction, to stave off every need and distress, to eliminate every sickness, and to remove every harm, even though He leaves His servants to be tried by disasters and hardships while the world is overflowing with disease, calamities, and tribulations, yet He is able to remove them all. [68] The merciful one certainly wants good for the one who receives mercy. Yet there is no evil in existence which does not contain some good within it, and were that evil to be eliminated, the good within it would be nullified, and the final result would be an evil worse than the evil containing the good. The certain amputation of a hand is an evident evil, yet within it lies an ample good: the health of the body. If one were to forego the amputation of the hand, the body would perish as a result—a worse evil still. So amputating a hand for the health of the body is an evil which contains good within it. But the primary intention which comes first in the consideration of one amputating is health—an unadulterated good. Yet since amputating the hand is the way to achieve it, amputation is intended for the sake of that good; so health was sought for itself first, and amputation second for the sake of the other and not for itself. They both enter into the intention, but one of them is intended for itself and the other for the sake of the first, and what is intended for its own sake takes precedence over that which is intended for the sake of the other: here the saying of God—great and glorious—is *a propos*: 'My mercy precedes My anger'.[8] His anger is His intending evil, so evil is by His intention, while His mercy is His intending good, [so good is by His intention]. But if He intended good for the good itself, yet intended evil not for itself but because there is some good within it; then good is accomplished essentially but evil is accomplished accidentally, and each according to divine decree. So nothing here goes against mercy at all.

The answer to your [problem] is that a small child's mother may be tender towards him and so keep him from undergoing cupping, while the wise father makes him do it by force.[9] An ignorant person thinks that the compassionate one is the mother rather than the father, while the intelligent understand that the father's hurting him by cupping reflects the perfection of his mercy and love as well as the completeness of his compassion; whereas the mother was his enemy in the guise of a friend, since a little suffering, when it is the cause of great joy, is not evil but good.

Now, if a particular evil occurs to you without your seeing any good beneath it, or should you think [69] it possible that a particular good be achieved without its being contained in evil, you should query whether your reasoning might not be deficient in each of these two trains of thought. As for saying that this evil has no good beneath it, minds simply are not up to knowing that. In this regard you are perhaps like a boy who saw cupping as nothing but an evil, or like the ignorant person who sees punishment by death as an unmitigated evil, because he is considering the particular qualities of the individual executed, for whom it is indeed a sheer evil, while overlooking the common good gained for the entire population. So he does not see that a particular evil leading to a public good is an unadulterated good: something which the good man ought not to overlook.

Or you should question your reasoning concerning the second train of thought, when you said that it was possible that this good be attained without being contained in that evil. Here too there is something obscure and subtle: the possibility or impossibility of everything possible or impossible cannot be perceived spontaneously nor by a simple survey, but may perhaps be known by an obscure, subtle discernment which the majority fails to reach.[10]

So accuse your reasoning in both these ways, and never doubt that He is *the most merciful of the merciful*, or that 'His mercy takes precedence over His anger', and never doubt that the one who intends evil for the sake of evil and not for the sake of good is undeserving of the name of mercy. Beneath all this lies a secret whose divulgence the revelation prohibits, so be content with prayer and do not expect that it be divulged.[11] You have been instructed by signs and given directions; so, if you are worthy of them, then ponder them!

You would have been heard
    Were you calling a living person,
But there is no life
    In the one you call. [70]

This is the condition of the majority—but I do not think that you, my brother, for whom this explanation is intended, lack the capacity to ponder the secret of God—great and glorious—in the divine decree, so all these hints and notices are unnecessary for you.

4. *Al-Malik*—the King—is the one who in His essence and attributes has no need of any existing thing, while every existing thing needs Him. There is nothing among things which can dispense with Him concerning anything—whether in its essence or its attributes, its existence or its survival; but rather each thing's existence is from Him or from something that is from Him. Everything other than He is subject to Him in its essence

and its attributes, while He is independent of everything—and this is what it is to be king absolutely.

*Counsel*: The creature cannot be conceived of as being king absolutely, for he cannot dispense with everything; indeed he will always be needy with regard to God the most high, and would be even if he were able to dispense with all but Him. Nor can one conceive of a creature having everything in need of him, since most existing things have no need of him. But to the extent that it is conceivable for one to be free from some things while other things need him, one may have a taste of kingship.

For a king among people is one whom no-one rules but God the most high, and who does not need anything except God—great and glorious. And with that he rules his kingdom insofar as his soldiers and his subjects obey him. Yet the kingdom proper to him is his own heart and soul, where his soldiers are his appetites, his anger, and his affections; while his subjects are his tongue, his eyes, his hands, and the rest of his organs.[12] If he rules them and they do not rule him, and if they obey him and he does not obey them, he will attain the level of a king in this world. And if that be coupled with the fact that he is independent of all people, yet all people are in need of him for their life now and in the future, he will be an earthly king. [71]

This is the level of the prophets—may God's blessings be upon all of them. For they have no need of direction to the next life from anyone except God—great and glorious—while everyone needs it from them. They are followed in this kingship by religious scholars, who 'inherit the legacy of the prophets'. Their kingship, however, is proportional to their ability to guide the people, and to their lack of need for asking for guidance.

By means of these attributes man comes close to the angels in qualities, and by means of them approaches God the most high. This kingship is a gift to man from the true king whose sovereignty has no competitor.

One of the 'knowers' [*ʿārifūn*] was right to respond to a prince who said to him: 'Ask me for what you need', by saying: 'Is that the way you speak to me when I have two servants who are your masters?' When he said: 'Who are these two?' the knower answered: 'Greed and desire: for I have conquered them yet they have conquered you; I rule over them while they rule you'. And one of them said to a certain shaykh: 'Advise me', and he said to him: 'Be a king in this world and you will be a king in the next'. When he said: 'How might I do that?' the shaykh answered: 'Renounce this world and you will be a king in the next'. He meant: detach your needs and your passions from this world, for kingship lies in being free and able to dispense with everything.

5. *Al-Quddūs*—the Holy—is the one who is free from every attribute which a sense might perceive, or imagination may conceive, or to which imagination may instinctively turn or by which the conscience may be moved, or which thinking demands. I do not say: free from defects and imperfections, for the mere mention of that borders on insult; it is bad form for one to say: the king of the country is neither a weaver nor a cupper, since denying something's existence could falsely imply its possibility, and there is imperfection in that false implication. [72]

I will rather say: the Holy is the one who transcends every one of the attributes of perfection which the majority of creatures thinks of as perfection. For creatures look first to themselves, become aware of their attributes, and realize that they are divided into (1) what is perfect regarding them, such as their knowledge and power, their hearing, seeing and speaking, their willing and choosing—so they employ these words to convey these meanings, and say that these are perfection terms. But the attributes also contain (2) what is imperfect regarding them, like their ignorance, debility, blindness, deafness, dumbness; and they employ these words to convey these meanings.

So the most they can do, in praising God the most high and qualifying Him, is (1) to describe Him by attributes taken from their perfection—from knowledge, power, hearing, seeing and speaking—and (2) deny of Him attributes taken from their imperfection. But God—may He be praised, the most High—transcends attributes taken from their perfection as much as He does those reflecting their imperfections. Indeed God is free from every attribute of which the created can conceive; He transcends them and above anything similar to them or like them. So if no authorization or permission had been given to use them, it would not be permissible to use most of these attributes. But you already understand what this means from the fourth chapter of the introductory part [Part One], so there is no need for repetition.

*Counsel*: The holiness of the servant lies in his freeing his knowledge and his will. He should free his knowledge from fanciful, tangible, and imagined things, and from all perceptions which he shares with animals. His continuing study and his ranging learning should rather be concerned with eternal divine things that are quite free from having to come closer to be perceived by the senses, or move farther away so as to be hidden from them. So he will become free himself from all tangible and imagined things, appropriating from the sciences what would remain were one deprived of [73] sensory organs and imagination, and so be refreshed by forms of knowledge that are noble, universal, and divine, concerned with eternal and everlasting objects of knowledge and not with changeable and imaginable individuals.

As for his will, he should free it from revolving around human participations that stem from the pleasure of desire or from anger, the enjoyment of food, sex, clothing, what can be touched or seen, or whatever pleasures come to him only by way of his senses and his body. In this way he will desire nothing but God—great and glorious; he will have no share except in God, no longing except to meet Him, no happiness except being near to Him. Even if paradise with all of its happiness were offered to him he would not turn his aspiration towards it, nor would the worlds [of heaven and earth] satisfy him, but only the Lord of these worlds.[13]

In sum, sensory and imaginary perceptions are shared with animals, and one should rise above them in favour of what is properly human. Animals also vie with man in human sensuous pleasures, so one should free oneself from them. The aspirant is as exalted as the object to which he aspires, as one who is intent on what enters his stomach is as valuable as what comes out of it, but whoever is intent on nothing except God—great and glorious—finds the level commensurate with his intent. And whoever elevates his mind above the level of imagined and tangible things, and frees his will from the dictates of passion, will lodge in the abundance of the garden of holiness.[14]

6. *Al-Salām*—The Flawless—is the one whose essence is free from defect, whose attributes escape imperfection, and whose actions are untarnished by evil; and given that He is like that, there is nothing flawless in existence which is not attributed to Him, and originates from Him. You already understand that the actions of the Most High are untarnished by evil; [74] that is, from un-adulterated evil intended for itself and not for the greater good [which lies] within it and is to be achieved from it. There is no actual evil answering to this description, as was indicated previously.

*Counsel*: Every servant whose heart is free from deceit, hatred, envy, and evil intent; and whose limbs are unblemished by sins and forbidden actions, and whose attributes are not affected by inversion and reversal, will be one who comes to God the most high *with a flawless heart*.[15] Among men, whoever comes close in characterization to that true and unadulterated Flawless One whose quality cannot be duplicated, may be considered to be flawless.

By an inversion of his attributes I mean that his reason will be imprisoned by his passion and anger, while the proper situation is the reverse of that: that anger and passion be imprisoned by reason and obey it. And if things are reversed there will be an inversion, as there is no well-being when the prince becomes a vassal or the king a subject. Nor can there be said to be well-being or 'Islam' unless 'someone protects the Muslims by his speech and his actions'.[16] And how can someone be described as flawless [or protector] who is not freed from his lower self?[17]

7. *Al-Mu'min*—the Faithful—is the one to whom security and safety are ascribed because He conveys the means to attain them and blocks the paths of dangers. For security and safety are only conceivable in locations of fear, and fear only arises with the possibility of annihilation, diminishment or destruction. The absolutely faithful one is God—may He be praised and exalted—as the one from whose direction alone security and safety may conceivably emanate. It is hardly a secret that someone who is blind in one eye fears that ruin may come to him inasmuch as he cannot see, yet his good eye keeps him safe from that. Or an amputee fears harm which can only be countered by the hand, [75] yet his sound hand protects him from it—and the same is true of all the senses and limbs, for the Faithful One created them, fashioning them and constituting them.

Let us suppose that a man is alone, pursued by a band of his enemies, cast down in ruin and unable to move his limbs because of his weakness. Even if he could move them, he has no weapons with him; or if he had weapons he could not prevail over his enemies alone; or if he had soldiers, he could not be sure that his soldiers would not be defeated. Nor has he a fortress to take refuge in. Then someone comes and attends to his weakness, strengthening him, providing him with soldiers and arms, and builds him a secure fortress, so granting him security and safety. It is fitting that such a one be named 'faithful' in his regard.

Man is basically weak by nature, subject to sickness, hunger and thirst from within; and to harm from burning, drowning, and from wounds and ferocious animals from without. The only one who can protect him from these fears is one who prepares remedies to counter and repell sickness, food to eliminate hunger and drink to slake the thirst, limbs to protect his body, and senses to gain information warning him from anything about to destroy him. Then there is his greatest fear—of eternal damnation—and nothing will protect him from that but the profession of faith in the unity of God. For God—may He be praised and exalted—guides him to it and makes him desire it, so that He says: '*"there is no god but God"*, is My fortress, and whoever enters into My fortress is safe from My punishment'.[18] For there is no security in the world unless it be derived from intermediaries which He alone creates and guides us in using. For He is the one *who gave unto each thing its nature and then guided it aright* (XX:50). He is truly the absolutely faithful one.

*Counsel*: A man's share in this name and attribute lies in all creatures' being safe from him. Moreover, every fearful person can anticipate help from him in keeping harm away from them, [76] whether in religious or worldly affairs. As the messenger of God—may God's blessing and peace be upon him—said: 'When one believes in God and the last day, his neighbour is safe from his misdeeds'.[19] Those men will be most worthy of the name 'faithful' who are instrumental in protecting a man from the punishment of God, by guiding him to the way of God—great and glorious—and directing him on the path of salvation. Now this is the vocation of prophets and scholars, and to that effect the messenger of God—may God's blessing and peace be upon him—said: 'Indeed you are rushing into the fire as moths flock to it, and I am pulling you back'.[20]

*Supposition and Counsel.* Perhaps you will say: in reality fear is from God the most high, for no one but He can make one fear. He is the one who makes His servants fear, and He created the causes of fear, so how can [giving] security be ascribed to Him? In answer to your question, [know that] both fear and security come from Him, for He is creator of the causes of security and fear alike. So the fact that He is the one who causes fear does not prevent Him from being faithful [i.e. the one who makes us safe], any more than His being the one who humbles keeps Him from being the one who honours—indeed He is both the Humbler and the Honourer [see names 25, 26]. Nor does His being the one who abases prevent His being the one who raises up, for He is both the Abaser and the Exalter [see names 23, 24]. Similarly, He is the faithful one and the one who causes fear, but divine instruction makes particular mention of 'faithful' and not of the 'one who causes fear'.

8. *Al-Muhaymin*—the Guardian—means with regard to God—great and glorious—the one who tends to His creatures with regard to their actions, their sustenance, and the time of their death. He tends to them by His cognizance, His possession, and His protection. Everyone who has complete command of a situation, who takes possession of it and protects it, will be its 'guardian'. Taking command comes down to knowledge, possession to the perfection of power, and protection to action. The one who unites these meanings is named guardian. But only God—great and glorious—joins them absolutely and perfectly, so it was said: it is one of the names of God the most high recorded in ancient writings.[21] [77]

*Counsel*: Every servant who watches over his heart until he supervises its depths and its secrets, and also takes possession of reforming his inner states and attributes, and undertakes to protect it continuously according to the requirements of his reform, will then be 'guardian' in relation to his heart. And if he extends his supervision and possession to undertaking to keep some servants of God—great and glorious—on the right way, after taking cognizance of their inner states and secrets by the way of clairvoyance [*tafarrus*] or inference from their behaviour, then his share in this meaning will be even more abundant and his portion greater.

9. *Al-ʿAzīz*—the Eminent—is one who is so significant that few exist like him, yet he is also one for whom there is intense need as well as one to whom access proves difficult. Unless these three meanings are combined, the term 'eminent' will not be used. There are many things in the world whose existence is rare, but if they are of little importance or not much use, they are not called 'eminent'. There are also many things whose significance is great, whose benefit is abundant, and whose equal does not exist, yet if access to them be not difficult, they are not called 'eminent'. The sun, for example, as well as the earth, have no equal. The benefit from each of them is abundant and the need for both is intense, but neither of them is described as 'eminent', because access to observing them is not difficult. So it is inescapable that all three meanings go together.

Moreover, in each of the three meanings there is perfection and imperfection. Perfection in rareness comes down to one only, for nothing is rarer than the one. And if it is one in the sense that any existence like it is impossible, only God the most high fulfills this sense. For even if the sun be one in actuality, it is not unique in possibility, for it is possible that one like it exist. Perfection in preciousness and in intensity of need means that all things need it in everything—for their very existence, their attributes, and their survival; and only God—great and glorious—fulfills that to perfection. Perfection [78] in difficulty of access lies in the impossibility of reaching

Him in the sense of comprehending His essence, and only God—great and glorious—fulfills that to perfection, as we have already explained that only God knows God. So He is truly and absolutely eminent, and nothing else is equal to Him in this.

*Counsel*: One is 'eminent' among people when God's people have need of him in matters most important to them, like the next life and eternal happiness. That is exceedingly rare and difficult to attain, except by those who hold the rank of prophet—may God's blessings be on all of them. Their eminence is shared with those who, in their time, are distinguished by being close to their level, like the caliphs, and the prophets' heirs among the scholars. The eminence of each one of them is in proportion to their elevation in rank above easy access and participation, and is measured as well by their concern for guiding creatures.

10. *Al-Jabbār*—the Compeller—is one who implements His will by way of compulsion in every single thing, yet no-one's will prevails over Him; He is the one from whose grasp nothing escapes, yet the hands of men do not reach to the sanctuary of His presence. The absolute compeller is God—may He be praised and exalted—for He compels each thing and nothing compels Him, and He has no competitor on either score.

*Counsel*: The compeller among men is one who is too high to be a follower and has attained the level of one followed; and is distinguished by the elevation of his rank in such a way that his life and his manner compels creatures to emulate him, and to follow him in his character and his conduct. For he benefits creatures but is not himself benefitted, he influences but is not influenced; he is followed but does not follow. No-one beholds him without ceasing to attend to himself, and becomes so totally absorbed in him so that he no longer attends to himself; nor does anyone aspire to sway him or to lead him. The master of men [Muḥammad]—may God's blessings and peace be upon him—enjoyed this attribute, [79] inasmuch as he said: 'Were Moses the son of ʿImrān alive he could not but follow me, for I am the master of Adam's offspring—and that is no boast'.[22]

11. *Al-Mutakabbir*—the Proud—is one who regards everything as unworthy of consideration in relation to himself, who sees greatness and majesty only in regard to himself, and looks upon others as a king looks upon his servants. And if his assessment be correct, he will truly be proud, and the one with this assessment will truly be proud. Moreover, that is absolutely inconceivable of anyone but God—great and glorious. But if that presumption of greatness were false and the one who considered himself incomparably great were not as he saw himself, then the pride would be false and reprehensible. In fact, should anyone regard himself in particular as majestic and great to the exclusion of all else, his assessment would be fallacious and his consideration vain—unless he be God—may He be praised and exalted.

*Counsel*: The proud among men is the 'knower' skilled in renunciation. The meaning of the knower's renunciation lies in freeing himself from whatever would distract his heart from the Truth and in disdaining everything but the Truth—may He be praised and exalted, thus despising both this world and the next, while removing himself from whatever in either one of them could distract him from the Truth most high. The renunciation of one who is not a 'knower', however, is but a transaction and a contractual arrangement: buying the good of the next world with the good of this one.[23] He renounces something now, hoping that it will be multiplied later, but this is only advance purchasing and bargaining. Whoever becomes a slave to the passion for food and sex is himself despicable, even were all that to last. The proud one despises every passion and gain that the beasts might conceivably share in. But God knows best!

12, 13, 14. *Al-Khāliq*—the Creator, *Al-Bāri'*—the Producer, *Al-Muṣawwir*—the Fashioner. It might be thought that these names are synonymous, and that they all refer to creating and inventing. But it does not need to be that way. Rather, everything which comes forth from nothing to existence needs first of all to be planned; secondly, to be originated according [80] to the plan; and thirdly, to be formed after being originated. God—may He be praised and exalted—is creator [*khāliq*] inasmuch as He is the planner [*muqaddir*], producer [*bāri'*] inasmuch as He initiates existence, and fashioner [*muṣawwir*] inasmuch as He arranges the forms of the things invented in the finest way.

This can be likened to building, for example, which requires an appraiser to estimate what he will need by way of wood, bricks, and land area, as well as the number of buildings with their length and their breadth. This latter is the responsibility of an architect, who will sketch and design them. Then it requires a builder responsible for the work which begins with the foundations of the buildings. Then it needs a decorator to chisel its exterior and to enhance its appearance, and someone other than the builder assumes this responsibility. This is what is customary in planning, building, and designing, but it is not like that in the actions of God—great and glorious. For He Himself is planner and originator and decorator—since He is the Creator, the Producer, and the Fashioner.

Another example is the fashioning of man, one of His creatures. His existence first requires a planning of that from which his existence [comes], for he is a body of a special kind. And the body is inevitably first, so that it may be characterized by attributes, as a builder needs tools if he is to build. Then the constitution of a man will not be sound without both water and earth. For earth alone is utterly dry and will not fold or bend [to make] movements, whereas water alone is utterly wet, so it neither holds together nor stands up, but rather spreads out. So it is inevitable that the wet be mixed with the dry to a proper balance, and the result is called clay.[24] Then it is necessary to have some heat to cook it until the mixture of water with earth be so constituted that it will not separate. For man is not fashioned from pure clay, *but from fired clay, like the potter's.* For pottery is clay turned into a paste by water which fire bakes until its mixture is properly constituted. Then we need to estimate a specific measure [81] of water and of clay, for if it be too little, for example, human actions will not result from it, but it will be on the scale of atoms and ants, so the wind will scatter it and the smallest thing destroy it. Nor does it require, for example, a mountain of clay, for that would exceed the amount needed: just enough—neither too much nor too little—in a proportion known to God—great and glorious.

Now all this resolves to planning, and He is Creator by virtue of planning these things, Fashioner by virtue of originating according to the planning, and Producer by virtue of sheer origination and invention from nothing into existence. For sheer origination is one thing, and origination according to plan is another. This is necessary for one to recall who eschews reducing creation to sheer planning, even though it has a certain linguistic rationale, since Arabs call a shoemaker a creator, for he estimates some layers of the shoe with respect to others. In that respect the poet says:

> You have indeed cut what you have created,
> While other people create but then do not cut.

As for the name 'Fashioner' [*al-Muṣawwir*], it belongs to Him inasmuch as He arranges the forms of things in the finest order, and forms them in the finest way. This is one of the attributes of action, and no one knows its essential reality except one who knows the form of the world in its totality, and then in detail. For the entire world is ruled by a single individual, and assembled from parts cooperating in discharging the obligations imposed upon each. For its members and its constituent parts are the heavens—the stars and the earths and whatever there is of water and air and the like which lies between them. Its parts are arranged in a highly organized fashion, so that if that arrangement were altered, the order would be abolished. What is specified to be above is what is fitting to be on high, while what is fitting to be below is in the lower part. Much as a builder places stones at the bottom of the walls and wood above them, not randomly but wisely and deliberately in order to make them firm. Whereas if that were reversed [82] and he were to place stones in the top of the walls and wood below them, the building would collapse, for its form would not have been able to stand up.

In like manner, one should understand the reason why the stars are on high while earth and water are below, as well as the kinds of order operative in the vast sectors of the universe. If we were to proceed to describe the regions of the universe and their details, and then remark on the wisdom in their assembly, the discussion would be too long. Everyone who has a more abundant knowledge of these details has a greater comprehension of the meaning of the name *al-Muṣawwir* [Fashioner].[25] And this arrangement and conception is found in every part of the world, however small, all the way to the ant and the atom and even in every one of the ant's organs. Indeed a prolonged discussion would be needed to explain the form of the eye, which is the smallest organ in an animal. Yet whoever does not know the layers of the eye and their number, their dispositions, shapes, capabilities, colours, and the sense of wisdom incorporated in them will neither know its form nor the One who forms them, except by a generic name. Similar things can be said of every form of each animal and plant; even of every part of each animal and plant.

*Counsel*: Man's share in this name lies in acquiring in his soul the form of existence of each thing with respect to its disposition and arrangement until he comprehends the organization of the universe and its arrangement throughout, as though he were [actually] looking at it; and then descends from the whole to details, looking on the human form, especially its body and bodily members, to come to know their kinds and number, their assembly and the wisdom in their creation and their arrangement. Then he will look into the intellectual attributes of the human form, and its higher powers by which [83] it knows and wills. In this way too he will know the form of animals and the form of plants, inside and out, according to his capacity, until the whole and its form are engraved in his heart. Now all of this stems from knowing the form of bodily things, and its compass is brief compared to knowing the arrangement of spiritual things, which includes knowledge—both generic and detailed—of the angels and their ranks, and how much is entrusted to each one of them in disposing the heavens and the stars, then in disposing human hearts by guidance and counselling, and finally in disposing animals by inspirations guiding them to satisfying their presumed needs.

Now this is man's share in this name: acquisition of the cognitive form corresponding to the existential form. For knowledge consists in a form in the soul corresponding to the thing known. The knowledge which God—great and glorious—has of the form is the cause of the form's existing in individuals, while the form existing in individuals is the cause of the cognitive form's being realized in the heart of man.[26] In that way man benefits by knowing the meaning of the name *al-Muṣawwir* [Fashioner] among the names of God—may He be praised and exalted, for by acquiring the form in his soul he also becomes a fashioner, as it were, even if that be put metaphorically. For in point of fact, these cognitive forms only occur within him by the creation of God the most high, and by His invention, not by one's own activity, but rather by one's striving to be exposed to the outpouring of the mercy of God the most high upon him. For God—great and glorious—*changes not what is in a people, until they change what is in themselves* (XIII:11). And thus the Prophet said—may God's mercy and peace be upon him—'Your Lord has gifts of His mercy for you throughout the days of your life; so expose yourselves to them'.[27]

Concerning the 'Creator' [*al-Khāliq*] and the Producer [*al-Bāri'*], man has no access to these names either, [84] except by a sort of remote metaphor, in the sense that creation and origination are based on the use of power according to knowledge, and God the most high has created knowledge and power for man, so that man has a way of achieving his potential in accordance with his estimation and knowledge.

Existing things are divided into (1) things whose realization does not depend at all on the power of people—like heaven and the stars, and earth with animals, plants, and the rest, and (2) things which are only realized by the power of people: whatever stems from the works of people, like crafts, politics, religious worship, and battles. And if man strives to prevail over himself by the disciplines appropriate to governing his soul and governing creatures, so that he reaches the point where he distinguishes himself by discovering things not discovered before, and he is thereby empowered to undertake them and interest others in them, he will be an inventor with regard to what did not previously exist. So it is said of the one who devised chess that he 'devised' and 'invented' it, because he devised what was not there before. However, the devising of something devoid of good is not among the attributes of praise.

Similarly, in religious exercises and disciplines, political activity and crafts which are a source of blessings, there are forms and institutions which some people learn from others, traceable, inevitably, to the first one who discovered or devised them. And since the one who devised them may be considered as the inventor of those forms and the creator planning them, it is legitimate to apply the name to him metaphorically.

Among the names of God most high, there are these predicated of men metaphorically, and they are the majority, while others are predicated of men literally and of God metaphorically—like 'patient' and 'grateful'. It is hardly appropriate that you notice the sharing in the name while overlooking this great difference which we have mentioned. [85]

15. *Al-Ghaffār*—He who is full of forgiveness—is the one who makes manifest what is beautiful and conceals what is ugly. Sins are among the ugly things which He conceals, by letting a cover fall over them in this world, and refraining from requiting them in the next. So forgiving is concealing.

The first concealing concerning man is that He made the ugly parts of his body, which the eyes find disgusting, to be enclosed inside it, covered over by the beauty of its exterior. How great a difference between the exterior of a person and his interior parts, in cleanness and uncleanness, in ugliness and beauty! Consider what it is that He makes manifest and what He conceals.

The second concealing consists in His having made the inmost part of man's heart the abode of his blameworthy thoughts and his ugly intentions so that no one can discover his secrets. For if people were to discover what occurs to one's mind in the course of his wicked thoughts, what deception and betrayal, or what evil thoughts concerning people be hidden in his conscience, they would detest him; indeed they would take steps to take his life and destroy him. Consider how one's secrets and weak spots are hidden from others!

The third concealing consists in His forgiving him the sins by which he deserves to be disgraced before all creatures. Indeed He has promised to *change one's evil deeds into good deeds*,[28] to cover one's disgusting sins with the merit of his good deeds if one dies as a believer.

*Counsel*: Man's share in this name lies in concealing concerning others what should be concealed regarding himself. As the Prophet said—may God's blessing and peace be upon him: 'whoever has concealed the weak spots of one of the faithful, God—great and glorious—conceals his weak spots on the day of resurrection'.[29] The slanderer, the prying person, and the one who repays [86] evil with evil are cut off from this attribute. In fact, the one who possesses this quality is one who makes public only what is best concerning God's creation. Every creature is bound to have perfection and imperfection or ugliness and beauty, so whoever overlooks the ugly and mentions the beautiful is one who shares in this attribute. So it is told of ʿĪsā [Jesus]—may God's blessings be upon him—that he and his disciples passed by a dead dog whose stench was overpowering, and they said: 'how this carcass stinks!' Yet ʿĪsā—may peace be upon him—said: 'what beautiful white teeth he has!'—so admonishing that what should be mentioned about everything is what is best in it.

16. *Al-Qahhār*—the Dominator—is the one who breaks the backs of the powerful among His enemies, and subdues them by killing and humiliation. Indeed there is no existing thing that is not subject to the domination of His power, and powerless in His grasp. That is all.

*Counsel*: The dominator among men is one who subdues his enemies. The greatest enemy of man is his soul, which is within him.[30] This soul is more of an enemy to him than Satan, of whose enmity he is wary. Whoever conquers the passions of his soul conquers Satan, since Satan lures him to ruin by means of his passions. One of Satan's snares is woman, and it is inconceivable that one who has lost the desire for women fall into this snare. Similarly, one conquers this passion under the influence of religion and the counsel of reason. Whosoever conquers the passions of the soul has conquered all men; no one has any power over him since the goal of his enemies is to try to annihilate his body, yet that person lives for his spirit. Whoever dies to his passion in his life will live in his death. [87] *Think not of those who are slain in the way of God, as dead. Nay, they are living. With their Lord they have provision. Jubilant are they. . .* (III: 169-70).

17. *Al-Wahhāb*—the Bestower. A gift is a present free from recompense and interests. If gifts with this qualification are numerous, the one giving them is called a 'bestower' and

'generous' soul. But generosity and giving cannot authentically be conceived of except from God the most high! For He is one who gives to everyone what he needs, neither for recompense nor out of interest, either now or later. But whoever bestows his gift with an eye to some interest to be realized by it sooner or later, be it appreciation, affection or release from blame, or acquiring distinction or mention—he is neither a giver nor generous, but rather engaged in transaction and recompense. Nor is all recompense something tangible received, but rather whatever one has not yet attained but intends as giver to attain by the gift is considered recompense. Whoever gives generously in order to gain distinction or praise for himself or to avert blame is engaged in a transaction. The truly generous is one from whom benefits pour forth on those who benefit from him, but not for a recompense returning to him. Indeed, whoever does something because he would have been denounced had he not done it is freeing himself by doing it; and that is interest and recompense.

*Counsel*: Generosity or giving *tout court* are inconceivable on the part of a human being. For did the performance not suit him more than refraining from it, he would not have undertaken it. So his initiative can be attributed to self-interest. But the one who sacrifices all that he owns, even his life, for the sake of God alone—great and glorious, not to arrive at the comfort of paradise or to avoid the pain of hell, or for an immediate or future gain such as would be accorded on being among the gains proper to man, such a one is worthy of being named giver and generous. [88] Below him is the one who gives freely to achieve the joy of paradise, and below him is the one who gives freely to obtain praise. Still, everyone who does not seek to receive tangible recompense will be called generous by those who think of recompense only in material terms.

If you say: the one who gives freely of all that he owns purely for the sake of God the most high, with no anticipation of gain now or later: how is he not generous, when he has no gain at all in it? We would say: his gain is God the most high: His acceptance, as well as meeting Him and reaching Him. And that is the happiness which man acquires by his free actions, and in comparison to it, every other gain is to be disdained.

Or you may say: what does it mean when they say that the 'knower' of God most high is one who worships God—great and glorious—for God's sake and not for the sake of an ulterior gain? For if human action is never free from gain, what difference is there between one who worships God most high purely for God and one who worships Him for some gain? You should know that according to the majority the expression 'gain' is equated with interests familiar to them, so whoever is free from those and retains no objective but God most high, will be said to be free from gain; that is, from what people reckon as gain. It is like their saying that the servant respects his master, not for the master's sake but for some gain coming to him from his master in the form of comfort or kindness. And the master looks after his servant, not for the servant's sake, but for some gain coming to him in the form of his service. As for the parent, he cares for his son for his son's sake, not for the gain coming to him from his son; indeed if there were no gain from him at all, he would still be concerned to look after him. [89]

Whenever one seeks something for the sake of something else and not for its own sake, it is as though he is not seeking that very thing. For that is not the goal which he is seeking; the goal he is seeking is something else. This is like the one who seeks gold. He does not seek it for its own sake but to attain food or clothes by it. Yet food and clothes are not sought for their own sake, but rather as a means to satisfy pleasure or ward off suffering. Now pleasure is sought for its own sake and not for another goal beyond it, and the case is similar regarding the avoidance of pain. So gold is a means to food, and food a means to pleasure, while pleasure is itself a goal and not a means to something else. Similarly, the son is not a means so far as the father is concerned, rather he seeks the well-being of the son for the sake of the son, because the child himself is his gain.

Similarly, whoever worships God—great and glorious—for the sake of paradise has made God—may He be praised and exalted—a means to seeking it rather than making Him the goal of his quest. The sign that something is a means is that no-one seeks it if its benefit can be attained without it, so that if one's intentions could be achieved without gold, gold would neither be loved nor sought, for what is really loved is the benefit sought and not the gold. So if paradise were attainable to one worshipping God for its sake, without worshipping God—great and glorious, he would not worship God. Therefore, what he is seeking and what he loves is paradise, and nothing else. Whoever has no love but God—great and glorious—and seeks nothing except Him, and whose gain lies in delight at meeting God most high, being near to Him, and in accompanying the heavenly host who are close to His presence; he is the one who can be said to worship God—great and glorious—for the sake of God; not in the sense that he is not seeking gain, but in the sense that God—great and glorious—is Himself his gain, and there is no gain beyond Him.[31]

Now whoever does not believe in the pleasure and delight in meeting God—great and glorious, or in knowing Him or seeing Him or drawing close to Him, will not long for Him; and whoever does not long for Him cannot conceivably have [90] that as his portion, since it is inconceivable that meeting God would be his goal from the beginning. For that reason, in his worship of God the most high, he will be like none other than an evil hireling, working only for the wage he anticipates from it. Most creatures have not tasted this pleasure nor have they known it, so they do not understand the pleasure of contemplating the face of God—great and glorious, but only believe in it insofar as they speak with their tongues. So far as their motivation is concerned, they are inclined towards the pleasures of meeting the black-and-white-eyed ones, believing in that alone.[32] You should understand from this that freedom from gain is impossible, if you allow that God the most high—that is, meeting Him and coming close to Him—may be called a gain. But if gain be equated with what the majority defines it to be, and what their hearts incline towards, then that is not a gain. Finally, however, if it be equated with something whose attainment serves man better than its absence, then it is a gain.

18. *Al-Razzāq*—the Provider—is the one who created the means of sustenance as well as those who are sustained, and who conveys the means to the creatures as well as creating for them the ways of enjoying them. Sustaining is of two kinds: outward, consisting of nourishment and food, which is for the sake of what is outward, namely the body. Inwardly, it consists in things known and things revealed, and that is directed to our hearts and inmost parts. This latter is the higher of the two modes of sustenance, for its fruit is eternal life; while the fruit of external sustenance is bodily strength for a short period of time. God—great and glorious—Himself attends to creating the two modes of sustenance and is graciously disposed to convey both kinds, but *He extends sustenance to whomever He wills and decrees* (XLII:12).

*Counsel*: The final result of a man's share in this attribute is two-fold. One of them consists in his knowing the essential reality of this attribute: that God alone—great and glorious—deserves it; so he expects sustenance only from Him, and does not rely on anyone but Him for it. As it is told of Ḥātim al-Aṣamm (the Deaf)—may God be merciful to him—when a man said to him: 'from where do you eat?' he said: 'from His storehouse'. The man [91] responded: 'does He hand sustenance down to you from heaven?' Ḥātim said: 'were the earth not His, He would have to hand it down from heaven'. To which the man said: 'What words you people speak!' And he responded:

'That is because nothing descends from heaven except words'. The man conceded: 'I am not strong enough to dispute with you'. So he said: 'That is because falsehood cannot prevail over truth'.[33]

The second result is that God grants him knowledge to give guidance, speech to bear witness and to teach, and hands to distribute alms; so that he may be a cause of higher sustenance reaching hearts by his words and deeds. For when God loves someone, then He makes creatures need that person more; and to the extent that he becomes an intermediary between God and men in enabling sustenance to reach them, will he acquire a share in this attribute. The messenger of God—may God's blessing and peace be upon him—said: 'the faithful steward who happily gives what he is ordered to is himself one of the almsgivers'.[34] Now the hands of men are the storehouses of God most high, so the one whose hand is made a storehouse for bodily sustenances, and his speech a storehouse of sustenance for hearts, has been honoured with a share of this attribute.

19. *Al-Fattāḥ*—the Opener—is the one by whose providence whatever is closed is opened, and by whose guidance whatever is unclear is disclosed. At times He opens kingdoms for His prophets and removes them from the hands of His enemies, saying: *Lo! We have given thee [O Muḥammad] a signal victory* (XLVIII:1) [literally: *We opened to you a signal opening*], and at other times He lifts the veils from the hearts of His holy men, opening to them the gates to the heavenly kingdoms and the beauties of His majesty. So He says: *That which* [92] *Allāh opens unto mankind of mercy, none can withhold it* (XXXV:2). Whoever has in his hands the keys to the invisible world and the keys to sustenance, it is proper that he be called an opener.

*Counsel*: Man should yearn to reach a point where the locks to the divine mysteries are opened by his speech, and where he might facilitate by his knowledge what creatures find difficult in religious and worldly affairs, for him to gain a share in the name of opener.

20. *Al-ʿAlīm*—the Omniscient: its meaning is evident. Its perfection lies in comprehending everything by knowledge—manifest and hidden, small and large, first and last, inception and outcome—and with respect to the multitude of objects known, this will be infinite. Then the knowledge itself will be the most perfect possible, with respect to its clarity and its disclosure, in such a way that no more evident disclosure or vision can be conceived. Finally it is not derived from things known; rather things known are derived from it.

*Counsel*: It is hardly a secret that man[35] has a share in the attribute of 'knower', yet man's knowledge is different from that of God the most high in three specific ways. First, regarding the multitude of things known: although the things man knows are wide-ranging, they are limited to his heart, and how could they correspond to what is infinite? Secondly, that man's disclosure, while clear, does not reach the goal beyond which no goal is possible; rather his seeing of things is like seeing them behind a thin veil. [93] You should not deny degrees of disclosure, because inward vision is like outward sight, so there is a difference between what is clear at the time of departure and what becomes clear in morning light.[36] Thirdly, that the knowledge which God—may He be praised and exalted—has of things is not derived from things but things are derived from it, while man's knowledge of things is contingent upon things and results from them.

Now if it is difficult for you to understand this difference, compare the knowledge of one who learns chess to the knowledge of the person who devised it. For the knowledge of the person who devised it is itself the cause of the existence of chess, while the fact that chess exists is the cause of the knowledge of one who learns it. The knowledge of the one who devised it precedes chess, while the knowledge of the learner follows upon it and comes afterwards. Similarly, the knowledge which God—great and glorious—has of things precedes them and causes them, while our knowledge is not like that.

Man's distinction is due to knowledge, inasmuch as it is one of the attributes of God—great and glorious; yet that knowledge is more distinguished whose objects are more distinguished, and the most distinguished object of knowledge is God the most high. Likewise, knowing God the most high is the most beneficial knowledge of all, while knowledge of the rest of things is only distinguished because it is knowledge of the actions of God—great and glorious, or knowledge of the way which brings man[37] closer to God—great and glorious, or the thing which facilitates attaining to knowledge of God the most high and closeness to Him. All knowledge other than that cannot claim much distinction.

21, 22. *Al-Qābiḍ, Al-Bāsiṭ*—He who contracts, He who expands—is the one who appropriates souls from dead bodies at death and extends souls to bodies at quickening. He also appropriates alms from the rich and extends sustenance to the weak. He extends sustenance to the rich to the point where no need remains, and holds it back from the poor until no strength is left. He contracts hearts and restricts them by what [94] He discloses to them of His exaltation and majesty and His lack of concern, while He expands them by what He makes available to them of His godliness, kindness and beauty.[38]

*Counsel*: The one who contracts and expands among men is the one who is inspired by marvels of wisdom and has been given comprehensiveness of speech. At times he expands the hearts of men by reminding them of the blessings of God—great and glorious—and His consolation, and other times he contracts them by warning them of the majesty of God and His greatness, and the varieties of His punishments, His scourge and His revenge on His enemies. As the messenger of God—may

God's blessings and peace be upon him—did when he shrank the hearts of the Companions from the desire for worship, by reminding them that God—great and glorious—said to Adam—may blessing and peace be upon him: 'On the day of resurrection I will raise up the portion of Hell', and he said: 'How many shall they be?' God said: 'Nine hundred and ninety-nine out of every thousand'.[39] The hearts of the Companions were broken so that they became lukewarm to worship. When he began to realize just how contracted and dispirited they were, he revived their hearts and expanded them by reminding them that in respect to the other peoples preceding them, they were like a black mole marking a white ox's hide.

23, 24. *Al-Khāfiḍ, Al-Rāfiʿ*—the Abaser, the Exalter—is one who abases infidels with damnation, and raises up the faithful by salvation. He exalts His holy people by bringing them closer, and abases His enemies by sending them far away. And whoever elevates his vision above tangible and imagined things, and his intention above blameworthy desires, God has raised him to the horizon of the angels close to Him [*muqarrabūn*]; while whoever restricts his vision to tangible things and his aspiration to the passions the beasts share with him, God will reduce him to the lowest of ranks. None but God most high does this, for He is the Abaser and the Exalter.

*Counsel*: Man's share in this consists in exalting the truth and abasing falsehood, by supporting those who are right and by reproaching those who are wrong, treating God's enemies as enemies in order to abase them, and befriending [95] God's friends in order to exalt them. As God the most high said to some of His friends: 'As for your renouncing the world, it has hastened the repose of your soul; and as for your mentioning me, you have been ennobled by it—but have you befriended a friend of mine or treated an enemy of mine as enemy?'[40]

25, 26. *Al-Muʿizz, Al-Mudhill*—the Honourer, He who humbles—is the one who gives dominion to whomever He wills and removes it from whomever He wills. True dominion consists in deliverance from the shame of need, the dominance of passion, and the disgrace of ignorance. The one from whose heart He removes the veil so that he can behold the beauty of His presence, and to whom He provides contentment so that he can thereby be freed from His creation, and whom He assists with power and support so that he can take charge of the dispositions of his own soul: he is the one whom God honours and to whom He gives dominion immediately. And He will honour him in the next life by bringing him closer and addressing him: *But ah! thou soul at peace! Return unto thy Lord content in His good pleasure! Enter thou among My bondsmen! Enter thou My garden* (LXXXIX:27-30).

The one whose eyes He extends over creatures until he comes to need them, and over whom He makes greed master to the point where nothing satisfies him, and whom by His deception He gradually brings to the point where he deceives himself and remains in the darkness of ignorance—he is the one whom God humbles and from whom He snatches dominion. And that is God's doing—great and glorious, as He wills and in the manner in which He wills, for He is the Honourer and He who humbles; He Honours whomever he wills and humbles whomever He wills. This humbled one is the one who is addressed and told: *but ye tempted one another, and hesitated and doubted, and vain desires beguiled you till the ordinance of God came to pass; and the deceiver deceived you concerning God. So this day no ransom can be taken from you* (LVII:14-15).This is ultimate humility. Every man who is used to facilitating the causes of honour by his action or speech, possesses a share in this attribute. [96]

27. *Al-Samīʿ*—the All-Hearing—is the one from whose perception nothing audible is removed, even if it be hidden. So He hears secrets as well as whispers, and even what is subtler and

more concealed than these; 'indeed He perceives the crawling of a black ant on a massive rock in the dark of night'. He hears the praise of those praising Him and rewards them, as well as the entreaties of those praying and responds to them. He hears without any auditory organs or ears, as He acts without limbs and speaks without a tongue; and His hearing is free from accidents which could befall it. When you elevate the All-Hearing above changes which happen to Him when audible sounds occur, and exalt Him above hearing by ears or by instruments and devices, you will realize that hearing, so far as He is concerned, is tantamount to an attribute by which the perfection of the qualities of things heard is disclosed. Whoever does not take care in considering this matter will inevitably fall into pure anthropomorphism. So be wary about it, and be precise when you consider it.

*Counsel*: Insofar as the senses are concerned, man has a share in hearing, but it is deficient. For he does not perceive everything audible but only sounds nearby; furthermore, his perception of them by means of organs and instruments is subject to deformity. If the sound is hidden it will fail to be perceived, or if it is far away it will not be perceived either, and if the sound is too loud the hearing may be destroyed so that it fades out.

A man's religious gain in this is two-fold. First, to realize that God—great and glorious—hears, so that he watches his tongue. Secondly, to know that He only created hearing for him to hear the word of God—great and glorious, and His book which He revealed so that man may receive from it the benefit of guidance to the way of God—great and glorious. So he will not use his hearing except for this. [97]

28. *Al-Baṣīr*—the All-Seeing—is the one who witnesses and sees in such a way that nothing is remote from Him, even what is under the earth. His seeing is also above having dependence

on pupils and eyelids, and exalted beyond reference to the impression of images and colours on His essence, as they are impressed on men's pupils, for that is a form of change and influence which requires coming-into-existence. Since He is above that, seeing in His case is equivalent to an attribute through which the perfection of qualities of visible things is disclosed. And that is clearer and more evident than what may be grasped by perception on the part of a sight limited to the appearances of visible things.

*Counsel*: As far as the senses are concerned, man's share in the attribute of sight is evident, yet it is weak and deficient since it does not reach to what is far away nor does it penetrate inside what is close at hand, but rather it deals with appearances and fails to reach what is interior and secret.

Yet one's religious gain from it is two-fold. First, to realize that He created sight for one to gaze upon the signs and wonders of the heavenly kingdoms and the heavens, so that his gazing will serve as an admonition. It was said to ʿĪsā [Jesus]—peace be upon him—'is any creature like you?' And he said: 'The one whose gazing serves as an admonition, whose silence is for reflection and whose speech is for remembering God—he is like me'. Secondly, to realize that one is seen by God—great and glorious—as well as heard, and not to underestimate His surveillance of him or His being informed about him. For whoever conceals from one who is not God what cannot be concealed from God certainly underestimates the surveillance of God—great and glorious, so fear of God is one of the fruits of believing in this attribute. How insolent and lost is the one who commits an act of disobedience when he knows that God—great and glorious—sees him, and how profane is the one who thinks that God the most high does not see him! [98]

29. *Al-Ḥakam*—the Arbitrator—is the arbitrating magistrate and the avenging judge, whose ruling no-one overturns and

whose decree no-one corrects. Among His rulings concerning men is that *man has only what he strives for, and that his effort will be seen* (LIII:39-40), and that *the righteous will meet happiness while the wicked will meet hell-fire* (LXXXII:13-14). His ruling regarding happiness to the righteous and misery to the wicked means that He makes righteousness and iniquity to be causes leading the one who possesses them to happiness or misery, as He makes medicines and poisons to be causes leading the one who receives them to recovery or death.

If the meaning of ruling is to arrange the causes and apply them to their effects, He will be an absolute arbitrator, because He is the one who causes all the causes, in general and in detail. Branching out from the arbitrator are the divine decree and predestination [*qaḍā' wa-qadar*]. His planning the principles positing the causes is so that this ruling may be applied to the effects. His appointing the universal causes—original, fixed and stable, like the earth, the seven heavens, the stars and celestial bodies, with their harmonious and constant movements which neither change nor corrupt—which remain without change until what is written be fulfilled (cf. II:235): this is His decree. As the most high said: *Then He ordained them seven heavens in two days and inspired in each heaven its mandate* (XLI:12). His applying these causes with their harmonious, defined, planned, and tangible movements to the effects resulting from them, from moment to moment, is His predestination. The ruling is the initial planning of the whole, together with the initial command which is like *the twinkling of an eye* (XVI:77). The decree is the positing of universal and constant causes. Predestination applies universal causes with their ordained and measured movements to their effects, [99] numbered and defined, according to a determined measure which neither increases nor decreases. And for that reason nothing escapes His decree and His predestination.

This cannot be understood without an example. Perhaps you have seen the horologe by which the times of prayer are announced. If you have not seen it, this much may be said of it in outline: there must be a device in it in the form of a cylinder containing a definite amount of water, and another hollow device placed in that above the water, with a string whose one end is tied to this hollow device while its other end is tied to the bottom of a small vessel placed above the hollow cylinder. In that vessel is a ball, and below it there is a shallow metal container placed in such a way that if the ball fell down from the vessel it would fall into the metal container and its tinkling would be heard. Furthermore, a hole of a definite size is made in the bottom of the cylindrical device so that the water runs out of it little by little. As the water level is lowered, the hollow device placed on the surface of the water will be lowered, thus pulling the string attached to it and moving the vessel with the ball in it with a movement which nearly tilts it over. Once it is tilted, the ball rolls out of it and falls into the metal container and tinkles. At the end of each hour, a single ball falls.

Now the separation between the two falls is determined by regulating the outflow of the water and its level, and that is done by determining the size of the hole through which the water flows. And that is known by way of calculation, since the amount of water coming out will be known and determined because the size of the hole has been determined by a known measure. So the level of the water lowers by that amount, thereby [100] regulating the descent of the hollow device, and so effectuating the string tied to it and initiating the movement in the vessel with the ball in it. All that is determined when its cause is determined, without increase or decrease. It is also possible that the falling of the ball into the container cause the next movement, and this movement cause a third, and so on through many levels to the point where remarkable movements are initiated by it, regulated by a defined measure. And their first cause is the outflow of water according to a definite amount. If you can picture this you should know that devising it requires three things. First of all, planning: the decision concerning what is needed regarding devices, causes, and movements leading to attaining what needs to be attained: that is the ruling. Secondly, creating these devices which are its fundamental constituents, and they are the cylindrical device containing the water, the hollow device placed on the surface of the water, the string tied to it, the vessel with the ball in it, and the container into which the ball falls: that is the decree. Thirdly, setting up a cause necessitating the determined, measured, and defined movement, and that is making a hole of a determined size in the bottom of the device so that when the water comes out of it, the movement in the water will lead to a movement in the surface of the water by lowering it, and thence to a movement in the hollow device placed on the surface of the water, then to a movement in the string, then to a movement of the vessel containing the ball, then to a movement in the ball, thence to the blow to the container when it falls into it, then to the tinkling which that effects, thence to alerting those present [101] and to their listening, and finally to their movements as they engage in prayers and actions once they know that the hour has come. And all of that will be according to a definite measure and an established plan, by reason of the regulation of all of it by the measure of the first movement, the movement of the water.

Now if you have understood that these devices are the fundamental constituents which are essential if there is to be movement, and that the movement must be regulated so that what is initiated from it is regulated also, you should be able to understand in a similar way how pre-determined events take place, none of which precedes or falls behind *when its appointed time comes* (LXIII:11); that is, once its cause is present. And all this takes place according to a definite plan, for *God brings His command to pass*, since *God has set a measure for everything* (LXV:3). For the heavens and the celestial bodies, the stars, the earth, sea, and air, and these large bodies of the universe are like those devices; while the cause of the movement of the celestial bodies and the stars, and the sun and the moon, according to a definite calculation is like the hole which sees to it that the water descends according to a definite measure. And the movement of the sun, moon, and stars flowing out to effect events on earth is like the effluent movement of the water to effect those movements which result in the ball's falling, and so informing people that the hour has come.

An example of the association of heaven's movements with changes on earth is given when the sun by its movements reaches its point of rising and shines over the world, so that people can see more easily, and it is easier for them to go out to their work. And when it reaches the west at sunset, those things become difficult for them, and they return home. When it nears the midpoint of the sky, its zenith above the heads of the people of the region, the air is heated and the summer heat becomes more intense, and fruit ripens. [102] When it moves beyond that point, winter comes and the cold intensifies. When it maintains a middle course we have moderate temperatures: spring comes, the earth germinates, and greenery appears. So, for the marvels you do not know, use an analogy with these everyday things you know to the marvels you do not know.

The differences among all these seasons are regulated by a known measure because they depend on the movements of the sun and moon. And *the sun and moon are calculated*, that is, their movements have a known measure. Now this is planning, while setting up universal causes is the decree; and the primary planning, which is *like the twinkling of an eye*, is the ruling. God the most high is a just arbitrator in these matters. As the movements of the device, the string, and the ball are not outside the will of the one devising the instrument, but are rather what he intended in devising the instrument; in a similar way no event which occurs in the world, be it evil or good, beneficial or harmful, is outside the will of God—great and glorious. Rather, they are the intention of God most high, for the sake of which He planned His causes, and this is the meaning of His saying: *For that He did create them* (XI:119).

Explaining divine matters by way of conventional examples is difficult, yet the aim of examples is to counsel. Leave the example aside and be alert to the objective, and beware of making likenesses and of anthropomorphism.

*Counsel*: You have understood from the example just mentioned how much of ruling, insight, decree, and planning man has, and that it is insignificant. In fact, what is important to him from all this consists in planning religious exercises and battles, and determining policies which lead to the well-being of religion and the world.[41] It is for that reason that God appointed His servants vicars on earth and settled them on it: *to watch over how they work.* [103]

The religious profit to be gained from beholding this attribute of God most high is to know that the matter is settled and not to be appealed. For the pen is already dry, [having written] what exists. The causes are already applied to their effects, and their being impelled towards their effects in their proper and appointed times is a necessary inevitability. Whatever enters into existence enters into it by necessity. For it is necessary that it exist: if it is not necessary in itself, it will be necessary by the eternal decree which is irresistible.[42] So man learns that what is decreed exists, and that anxiety is superfluous. As a result he will act well in seeking his livelihood, with a tranquil spirit, a calm soul, and a heart free from disruption.

But you may say: two ambiguities arise from it. First, how can anxiety be superfluous when it is also decreed? For a cause has been determined for it and once its effect occurs, it is necessary that anxiety be realized. The second raises the question: if the matter is already settled, why work, when the cause for happiness or distress has already been settled? The answer to the first question is that their saying: 'what is decreed exists and anxiety is superfluous', does not mean that it is superfluous in the sense that it is outside all determination, but rather that it is itself superfluous—that is, useless nonsense, for it will not cancel what is decreed. It is pure ignorance to let something whose occurrence is expected be a cause for distress, because if its occurrence is decreed, then neither caution nor anxiety can cancel it. It is like hastening some sort of pain out of fear of pain's occurring. And if its occurrence is not decreed, there will be no sense worrying about it, so in both of these respects anxiety is superfluous.

As for work, the Prophet's answer to that was in his saying—may God's blessings and peace be upon him: 'Work, for the path is made easy for everyone [104] towards what he was created for'.[43] This means that for whomsoever happiness is ordained, it is determined by a cause, and its causes become easy: to wit, obedience. And for whomsoever misery is determined—God forbid!—it is determined by a cause, and that is one's indolence with regard to pursuing its causes. And the cause for his indolence might be what is settled in his mind: 'If I am destined for happiness, there is no need to work, and if I am to be miserable, there is no point in working'. But that is foolishness, for he does not realize that if he is to be happy, he would only be happy because the causes of happiness, like knowledge and work, would come to him, and if they are not within his reach and do not come to him, that is an indication of his misery.

For a similar case take someone who wants to be a jurisprudent and reach the rank of *imām*. If it is said to him: work hard, learn, and persevere! he will say: 'If God—great and glorious—decreed from eternity for me to be an *imām*, then no effort will be needed; yet if He decreed for me to be ignorant, then no effort is required'. He should be told: 'If He gave this thought power over you, it shows that He has decreed for you to be ignorant'. If He decreed eternally for someone to be an *imām*, He decreed it in its causes, so that the causes will come to him, and He will dispose him by means of them, and He will remove thoughts from him which would lure him to discouragement or idleness. Indeed, the one who makes no effort will not achieve the rank of *imām* at all, whereas for the one who strives and finds its causes within his reach, his hope of attaining it will come true if he continues his efforts to the end and encounters no obstacles which block the way. From this you should understand that no one attains happiness except those *who come to God with a sound heart.* Soundness of heart is a quality acquired by effort, like understanding oneself and the quality of being an *imām*—and there is no difference between them! [105]

Of course in beholding the Arbitrator, people are at different levels. There are some who regard the end considering how [life] will end for them, and some who regard the beginning considering how it was decreed for them in eternity. The latter are higher because the end is contingent upon the beginning. Some take leave of past and future, and are sons of the moment [*ibn waqtihi*], for they contemplate Him, happy with the result of the predestination of God—great and glorious—and what appears of it, and these are higher than the ones preceding. Then there are some who take leave of present, past and future, whose hearts are absorbed in the Arbitrator, clinging to their vision of Him, and this is the highest level.[44]

30. *Al-ʿAdl*—The Just—means one who is just, and He is one from whom just action emanates, the opposite of injustice and oppression. One cannot know one who is just without knowing his justice, and one cannot know his justice without knowing his action. So whoever wants to understand this attribute must comprehend the actions of God most high from the kingdoms of the heavens to the ends of the earth, to the point where one does not notice *any fault in the creation of the infinitely good One*, and turns again and sees no rifts in it, yet turns one more time only *to have his sight become weak and dulled;* for the beauty of the divine presence has overwhelmed him and bewildered him with its harmony and its regularity: for such a

man, something of the meaning of His justice—the most high and holy One—clings to his understanding.[45]

He created the categories of existing things, the physical and the spiritual, the perfect and imperfect among them; *and He gave to each thing its created existence,* in which He is *generous,* and also ordered them in a placement suitable to them, in which He is *just.* Among the large bodies of the universe are the earth, water, air, the heavens and the stars, and He created them and ordered them, placing the earth lowest [106] of all, putting water above it and air above the water and the heavens above the air. And if this arrangement were to be reversed, the order would be untenable.

An explanation expounding the merits in justice of this order and arrangement would probably be difficult for many to understand. So let us come down to a popular level and consider man in his body. It is composed of diverse members as the universe is composed of diverse bodies. An initial way of dividing it regards His composing man from bone, flesh, and skin. He placed bone as an internal support with flesh enclosing it to protect it, and skin enclosing and protecting the flesh. Were this order to be reversed so that what is within were to be on the outside, the arrangement would be untenable.

And if this be obscure to you, then consider that He created diverse members for man, like hands, feet, eyes, nose, and ears. By creating these members He is generous, and by placing them in their particular placement He is just. For He put the eyes in the place most suitable in the body: if He had created them in the back of the head or on the feet or hand or on the top of the head, the resulting shortcomings, as well as the damage to which they would be exposed, would be evident. In similar fashion He suspended the hands and arms from the shoulders, and had He suspended them from the head or the loins or the knees, the imbalance resulting from that would be evident. Similarly, He placed all the senses in the head to oversee the rest of the body since they are there to reconnoitre. For if He had placed them in the feet, their arrangement would be completely upset. Such an explanation [107] for every organ would prolong our account, so what you should know, in short, is that nothing has been created except in the placement intended for it. For if it were placed to the right or to the left of where it is, or below or above it, it would be deficient or useless, ugly or disproportionate, and repugnant in appearance. So the nose was created in the middle of the face; were it fashioned on the forehead or on the cheek, such a defect would reduce its usefulness. Perhaps your understanding has been enhanced enough to perceive the wisdom of this.

You should also know that He did not create the sun in the fourth heaven, that is, in the middle of the seven heavens, in jest. Rather He created it aright, placing it in a position suitable to it alone, so that it could achieve its purposes. Yet perhaps you might fail to perceive the wisdom in it because you have reflected but little on the kingdoms of the heavens and earth and their wonders. Were you to contemplate them, the wonder you would see there would outstrip the wonders of your body. And how could it not be so, when *the creation of the heavens and earth is greater than the creation of people.* Would that you had extensive knowledge of the wonders of your soul, and devoted yourself to contemplating them as well as the bodily parts enclosing them, so you would be among those of whom God—great and glorious—says: *We shall show them our portents on the horizons and within themselves* (XLI:53). How could you be among those of whom God said: *Thus did we show Abraham the kingdoms* [108] *of the heavens and the earth* (VI:75)? Can the gates of heaven be opened to one preoccupied with concerns of the world and enslaved to greed and passion?

Now this offers some symbolic indication of how to understand the first steps along the way to knowing this one name. For its explanation would require volumes, as with the explanation of the meaning of every one of these names. For nouns derived from verbs will not be understood without first understanding the actions,[46] and everything in existence comes from the actions of God most high. So whoever fails to grasp them, either in detail or in general, will have no part of them except for mere issues of language and commentary. Now one cannot hope for a knowledge of them in detail, for there is no end to that. Yet man does have a way to a general knowledge of them, and his share in the knowledge of the names is proportional to the extent of his general knowledge of actions, and that involves the gamut of all forms of knowledge. The aim of a book such as this, however, can only be to offer pointers as keys to finding how the whole might be joined together.[47]

*Counsel*: Man's share in justice is well-known. First, there is the justice he has to have concerning his own attributes, and that consists in his putting passion and anger under the guidance of reason and religion; for as soon as he puts reason at the service of passion and anger, he will certainly commit injustice. This is the sum total of justice in oneself, and its particular implications consist in observing all of the parameters of the Law. So his justice regarding all of his members lies in his using them according to the ways which the Law permits. Moreover, his duties in justice towards his family and relatives; or, if he is a sovereign, concerning his subjects, are well-known.

Now one may think that injustice is to cause harm, and that justice consists in bestowing benefits on people, but this is not the case. For were the king to open his storehouses filled with arms [109] and books and varieties of goods, yet distribute money to the wealthy and grant arms to scholars, handing over fortresses to them also; while he distributed books to the troops and combat personnel, handing over mosques and schools to them as well, it would indeed be a benefit to them but it would just as certainly be oppressive and a departure from justice, since he would have put everything in a place inappropriate to it. But were he to harm the sick by making the drinking of medicines, bleeding, or cupping compulsory; or harm the criminal by punishment of death or amputation or beating, he would be just because he put them in their proper place.

Man's religious gain from his believing that God—great and glorious—is just lies in not taking objection to Him in His plan, His decree, and all of His actions, whether they correspond to His will or not. For all of that is just: it is as it should be and how it should be. Were He not to do what He did, something else would have happened which would be much more harmful than what did happen, as the sick person who did not submit to cupping would suffer with a pain greater than the pain of cupping. This is the way God most high is just, and faith in Him cuts short objections and resistance, both outward and inward. The perfection of faith consists in 'not cursing fate', not attributing things to the influence of celestial bodies, and not taking objection to Him, as it is customary to do; but rather in knowing that all of this takes place by causes subservient to Him, themselves ordered and directed to their effects in the best order and direction, according to the highest standpoint of justice and benevolence.

31. *Al-Laṭīf*—the Benevolent. One is deserving of this name if one knows the subtleties of those things which are beneficial, as well as their hidden aspects, along with what is subtle about them and what is benevolent. Moreover, in conveying them to those who are deserving, he is committed to the path of gentleness rather than harshness. For the perfect meaning of 'benevolent' combines gentleness in action with a delicacy of perception [110]. Such perfection in knowledge and action is inconceivable except in God—may He be praised and exalted. His comprehending the subtleties and hidden aspects cannot be detailed; rather what is hidden is exposed to His knowledge as though it were manifest, with no distinction between them. As for His being gentle and benevolent in actions, it too cannot be reckoned: indeed one only knows what the benevolence in action is from knowing His actions, and the subtleties of

gentleness found in them. In the measure that one's knowledge of them expands, knowledge of the meaning of the name 'The Benevolent' is increased. Explaining that would require going on at length, and even then it is inconceivable that many volumes would satisfy a tenth part of a tenth of it, but it is possible to advise regarding some aspects of its total arrangement.

An example of His being benevolent is His creating the foetus in the womb of its mother, in a threefold darkness, and His protecting and nurturing it through the umbilicus until it separates and becomes independent by taking food through its mouth; and then His inspiring it upon separation to take the breast and suckle it, even in the darkness of night, without any instruction or vision. Moreover, He makes the shell burst for the sake of the little bird, and inspires it to pick up grains immediately. Then there is the delay in creating teeth from the outset of a creature's existence until the time they are needed, since it has no need of teeth while it is being nourished by milk, but He makes them come in afterwards when it needs to crush food. Then there is the differentiation of teeth into molars for crushing, canine teeth for breaking, and sharp-edged middle incisors for cutting. Then there is the use of the tongue, whose more obvious purpose is verbal articulation, to direct the food to be crushed as though it were a shovel. The explanation of His benevolence will not be exhausted even by noting how it provides a morsel for man to eat without his suffering any discomfort while [111] a countless number of creatures cooperate to make it suitable: those who reclaim the land, plant the seed, water it, harvest it, sift it, grind it, knead it, and bake it, and the rest.

In sum, He is wise insofar as He plans things,[48] generous insofar as He creates them, fashioner insofar as He orders them, just insofar as He puts each thing in its proper place, and benevolent insofar as He does not overlook subtleties and qualities of gentleness concerning them. Whoever fails to discern the effects of these actions will certainly miss the true meaning of these names.

An example of the way He is benevolent towards His servants is His giving them more than they need and His demanding of them less than they are capable of. It also pertains to His being benevolent to facilitate their attaining the happiness of eternity with little effort in a short time, that is, a lifetime; for there is no way of comparing that with eternity. The production of pure milk out of digested food and blood, as well as the production of precious gems from hard stone, of honey from the bee, silk from the worm, and pearls from the oyster—are all part of His benevolence. But even more amazing than that is His creating from impure semen one who is a vessel for His knowledge, bears His trust and witnesses to His heavenly kingdoms—this too is impossible to reckon.

*Counsel*: A man's share in this attribute is gentleness with regard to the servants of God—great and glorious, and a predilection for them in petitioning God the most high; as well as guiding them to the happiness of the world to come in a manner free from rebuke or harshness, fanaticism or disputation. The best way of being benevolent open to man lies in attracting others to accept the truth by one's good qualities, pleasing comportment, and exemplary actions, for they are more effective and more benign than eloquent exhortation. [112]

32. *Al-Khabīr*—The Totally Aware—is one from whom no secret information is hidden, for nothing goes on in the realms of heaven or earth, no atom moves, and no soul is stirred or calmed, without His being aware of it. It has the same meaning as 'the Omniscient', yet when knowledge [*ʿilm*] is related to hidden secrets it is called 'awareness' [*khibra*], and the one who possesses it is 'He who is aware [of everything]'.

*Counsel*: Man's share in this name lies in his being aware of what goes on in his world. His world is his heart, his body, and the hidden things by which his heart is characterized: deception and treachery, preoccupation with earthly things, harbouring evil intent while putting on a good front, or adopting a decorous show of sincerity while being devoid of it. Only one who is extremely experienced knows these characteristics: one who is aware of his lower self and experienced in it, who knows its deceit, its deluding, and its ruses, so that he is on his guard against it and has gone to work to oppose it, adopting a watchful vigilance over it. Among men such a one deserves to be called 'totally aware'.

33. *Al-Ḥalīm*—the Mild—is one who observes the disobedience of the rebellious and notices the opposition to the command, yet anger does not incite him nor wrath seize him, nor do haste and recklessness move him to rush to take vengeance, although he is utterly capable of doing that. As the Most High said: *If God should take men to task for their wrongdoing, He would not leave on the earth one creature that crawls* (XVI:61).

*Counsel*: Man's share in the attribute of 'mildness' is evident, for mildness is among the fine qualities of men, so it would be superfluous and prolix to explicate.

34. *Al-ʿAẓīm*—the Tremendous.[49] You should know that in its first imposition the term 'tremendous' applies only to bodies. For it is said: 'this body is tremendous', or 'this body is more tremendous than that body' if it is [113] more extended than the other in its parameters of length, width, and depth. 'Tremendous' is then divided into (1) what fills the eye and captures its attention, and (2) what sight cannot conceivably encompass in all of its extremities, such as earth and heaven. So an elephant is tremendous, but sight can certainly encompass its extremities; therefore it is tremendous by comparison to what is smaller than it. So far as the earth is concerned, however, it is inconceivable that sight encompass its extremities, and so with the heavens. This is the absolutely tremendous with regard to visual perception.

Moreover, you should realize that there are differences as well among the objects of intellectual perception: some of them intellects can comprehend in their essential reality, while in the case of others intellects fall short of that. And those of which intellects fall short are divided into (a) what some intellects may conceivably comprehend while most fall short of comprehending them, and (b) what it is inconceivable in principle that any intellect could comprehend in its essential reality; the absolutely tremendous which exceeds every intellectual limit so that comprehending its essence is inconceivable, namely, God most high, as we have already explained in the first Part.

*Counsel*: Among men it is prophets and scholars who are tremendous, so that when a wise man knows something of their attributes his heart is filled with awe; in fact, his heart so overflows with awe that no room is left for anything else. A prophet is tremendous with respect to his community, a master [*shaykh*] with respect to his disciple, and a professor with respect to his student, whose intellect falls short of comprehending the range of his master's attributes. For if he were equal to him or surpassed him, the master would no longer be tremendous by comparison with him. Still, every use of 'tremendous' assigned to something other than God—great and glorious—falls short of being absolutely tremendous, for it is manifested by comparison of one thing [114] below another. The *tremendum* of God most high is the exception, for He is tremendous absolutely, not through comparison.

35. *Al-Ghafūr*—the All-Forgiving—relates to the meaning of 'the One who is full of forgiveness' *(al-Ghaffār)*, yet it bespeaks a kind of amplitude which 'He who is full of forgiveness' does not convey. For 'He who is full of forgiveness' represents an emphatic form derived from 'forgiveness', connected to repeated forgiveness one time after another, as *al-faᶜᶜāl* bespeaks a great deal of activity [*fiᶜl*] while *al-faᶜūl* conveys its excellence,

perfection, and completeness. He is all-forgiving in the sense that He is the perfection and completeness of forgiveness and forgiving, to the point of reaching the highest level of forgiveness. Moreover, the discussion of this has already taken place [cf. §15].

36. *Al-Shakūr*—the Grateful—is the one who rewards the practice of a few pious deeds many-fold, and, in response to the actions of a few days, gives limitless happiness in the life to come. The one who rewards a good deed many-fold is said to be grateful for that deed, while whoever commends the one who does a good deed is also said to be grateful. Yet if you consider the multiplication factor in reward, only God—great and glorious—is absolutely grateful, because His multiplication of the reward is unrestricted and unlimited, for there is no end to the happiness of paradise. God—may He be praised and exalted—says *Eat and drink with wholesome appetite for that which you did long ago, in days gone by* (LXIX:24).

If you go on to consider the factor of praise, the praise we give is to someone else, yet when God—great and glorious—praises the works of His servants, He praises His own work, for their works are His creation. And if the one who is given something and goes on to praise is thankful, then whoever gives and then praises the recipient is even more deserving of being called grateful. So the praise of God the most high for His servants is like His saying: *Men and women who remember God often* (XXXIII:35); and also like His saying *how excellent a servant he was! he was penitent* (XXXVIII:30)—and similar things [115]. And all this is a gift from Him.

*Counsel*: It is conceivable that man[50] be grateful with respect to another man, at one time in praising him for having done good deeds to him, at another by rewarding him with more than the other has done for him, and that is a praiseworthy quality. The Messenger of God—may God's blessing and peace be upon him—said: 'whoever does not thank men does not thank God'.[51] Yet so far as man's thanking God—great and glorious—is concerned, it can only be done by extension and in a metaphorical way. For it is such that, if man praises, his praises are inadequate, 'for the praise due Him is beyond reckoning'. And if he renders obedience, his obedience is another blessing from God to him; indeed his gratitude itself is another blessing following the blessing for which he gives thanks. And the best form of gratitude for the blessings of God—great and glorious—is to put them to use, not in disobeying, but in obeying Him. Yet even that comes about by the success given by God in His facilitating man's being grateful to his Lord.

Conceiving this properly requires a subtle discussion, and we have elaborated it in the 'Book of Thanksgiving' in the *Revival of the Religious Sciences* [*Iḥyā' ʿUlūm al-Dīn*], where one may inquire about it since this book does not have room for it.[52]

37. *Al-ʿAlī*—the Most High—is the one above whose rank there is no rank, and all ranks are inferior to Him. This is because 'high' is derived from 'height', and 'height' is taken from elevation that is the opposite of lowness: be that according to a perceptible ranking, as in a grade or a staircase, where all bodies are placed one above the other; or by a rational ranking of objects ranked according to kinds by a rational ordering. Everything which has the quality of being *above* in place has spatial elevation, and everything which is *above* in rank has elevation in rank. Moreover, rational gradings are understood like perceptible gradings: an example of rational grades being the difference between reason and result, [116] cause and effect, agent and recipient, perfect and imperfect. Once you have determined a thing, it is a cause of a second thing, and that second thing cause of a third, and the third of a fourth—up to ten steps, for example—the tenth occurs in the last rank, and it is the lowest, the most inferior cause. The first occurs in the first rank according to causality, and it is the highest. So the first

is above the second—*above* in meaning, not in place, and height is identical with the quality of being *above*.

If you understand the meaning of rational gradings, you should know that objects cannot be divided into diverse grades according to reason, without the Truth—may He be praised and exalted—being in the highest grade of the diverse grades, to the point where it is inconceivable that a grade be above Him—for He is the absolute high one. Everything other than Him is high by comparison with what is below it, and is inferior or low by comparison with what is above it.

An example of rational division can be found in objects' being divided into causes and effects, so that the cause is above the effect—*above* in rank; yet only the cause of causes is *above* absolutely. Similarly, existing things are divided into animate and inanimate, and animate things are divided into those having only sensible perception [animals] and those which have rational as well as sensible perception. Those which have rational perception are divided into those in which passion and anger resist what they know [men] and those whose perception is free from such troubling opposition, while those who are free are divided into what can be afflicted but are endowed with safekeeping from this, like the angels, and what is impossible to be afflicted, which is God—may He be praised and exalted. Now it should be evident to you from this division and grading that angels are above men, men above animals, and God—great and glorious—is above everything, for He [117] is absolutely high. He is the living and the life-giver, the absolute knower, creator of scholars' knowledge, transcending every kind of imperfection. Indeed, the inanimate are assigned to the lowest grades of the grades of perfection, while nothing is assigned to the other side but God the most high, and this is the way you should understand His being above and His height.

These names are posited first in relation to visual perception, which is the level of common folk. Then when the elite became aware of intellectual perception and found parallels between it and sight, they borrowed from sight the designated words; and the elite understood them and grasped them, while they were rejected by common folk whose perception does not go beyond the senses, which is the level of animals. For they only understand immensity in spatial terms, height in terms of place, and *above* in similar terms. Now if you understand this, then you have understood the meaning of His being above [i.e., on] the throne. For the throne is the most exalted body, and is above all bodies: an object far beyond determination and calculation in terms of the boundaries of bodies and the measure proper to them; it is above all bodies in rank. Special mention is made of the throne because it is above all bodies, so that what is above [i.e. on] it is above all of them. This is like the saying: the caliph is above the sultan, so advising us that if he is above the sultan he is above all the people who are themselves below the sultan.

One wonders how one of the Ḥashwiyya,[53] who only understand *above* in terms of place, would respond if he were asked how two distinguished individuals sit in rank and in official assemblies. He might say that 'this one sits above that one', knowing that he only sits at his side. [118] For he would only be seated *above* him if he were seated on his head, or in a place built above his head. Yet if one said to him: 'You are lying, for he is not sitting above him nor below him but beside him;' he would disown any such denial and say: 'What I mean by that is *above* in rank, and proximity to the highest position in the house, for the one closer to that position which is the furthest point is *above* by comparison with the one farther from it'. Yet he does not understand from this that every ordering has two extremes, such that one can apply the term 'above' or 'high' to one extreme, and its opposite to the other.

*Counsel*: It is inconceivable that man be absolutely high, since he does not attain any rank without there being a higher one in existence, namely the ranks of prophets and of angels. Of course, it is conceivable that one attain the rank such that there is none above it among people, and that is the rank of our prophet Muḥammad—may God's blessing and peace be upon him. Yet even he falls short by comparison with the absolute height, since he is high by comparison with some existing things. Yet because he is high by comparison with what in fact exists, and not by way of necessity, his existence might be accompanied by the possible existence of a man above him. Now the absolutely most high has the quality of being above not comparatively but necessarily, that is, not in relation to an existing thing which might be associated with it as a possible contrast. Enough!

38. *Al-Kabīr*—the Great—is one who possesses greatness [*kibriyā'*], where greatness is identical with the perfection of essence, and by 'perfection of essence' I mean perfection of existence. Now perfection of existence resolves to two things: first, His enduring in an everlasting and eternal manner. For every existing thing bounded by non-existence preceding or following it is imperfect. So a man is said to be great when the span of his existence is long, that is, [119] 'great of tooth'—enduring for a long time, yet he is not said to be 'tremendous [*ʿaẓīm*] of tooth'. So 'great' is used in situations where 'tremendous' is not used. Now if one whose span of existence is long may be called 'great', even though the span of his enduring be limited, the one whose enduring is everlasting and eternal, and to whom non-existence is impossible, is even more deserving of being 'great'. Secondly, His existence is that existence from which emanates the existence of every existing thing. So if the one whose existence is perfected in itself is said to be perfect and great, the one from whom existence pours forth to all existing things is even more deserving of being perfect and great.

*Counsel*: He is great among men whose attributes of perfection are not restricted to him but flow out to others, so that he will not keep company with anyone without pouring forth on him some of his perfection. Man's perfection lies in his reason, his piety, and his knowledge; the great man is the scholar who guides mankind, and the one who is fit to be a model from whose knowledge and brilliance others will learn. In that respect, ʿĪsā [Jesus]—peace be upon him—said: 'the one who knows and acts is the one who is called tremendous [*ʿaẓīm*] in the kingdom of heaven'.

39. *Al-Ḥafīẓ*—the All-Preserver—is the perfect preserver [*ḥāfiẓ*]. But this will not be understood until the meaning of 'preservation' is understood, and that is achieved in two ways. First, perpetuating the existence of existing things and sustaining them, the opposite of which is annihilation. God the most high is the preserver of the heavens and earth, the angels and existing things—whether they last a long time or not, as with animals, plants, and the rest. [120] The second way—which is the more evident of the two—consists in preserving by safeguarding from each other those things which are inimical to or at odds with each other. What I mean by this is the mutual enmity between fire and water, for these two are inimical to one another by nature. Either water extinguishes fire, or if the fire prevails, it transforms water into steam and thence into air. The opposition and enmity is evident between heat and cold since one of them prevails over the other, and similarly between wet and dry. The rest of earthly bodies are composed of these mutually inimical elements: for it is clear that animals have such a need of natural heat that their life would expire were it to cease, and that they require liquid to nourish their bodies, as with blood and like fluids; but they also need dryness to hold their parts together, especially those which are hard, like the bones. Or cold is needed to temper the severity of the heat so that the mixture may be moderated and not burned, and so that bodily liquids are not quickly dissolved. These are mutually inimical elements contending with one another.

God—great and glorious—reconciles these opposing and contending elements within the skin of man and the body of animals, plants, and the rest of composite things. For were He not to preserve them, they would clash and separate, so that their mutual coherence would cease and their orderly arrangement disappear, along with the abstraction which they have become ready to receive by virtue of their orderly arrangement and coherence. God the most high preserves these things, now by moderating their powers, or at another time by assisting what has been overpowered. Moderation occurs when the power of cold is similar in extent to the power of heat, so that when they come together one of them does not overpower the other, but they rather contend with one another, since no one of them is worthier to overcome than to be overcome. The two stand against each other and the consistency of the composite thing is maintained by their standing against one another or their balance. This is what is given the designation: temperance of physical constitution.[54] [121]

Secondly, there is His providing for the one of the two contraries which was overcome, reviving its strength to the point where it can stand against what overcame it. For example, heat invariably consumes moisture and dries it up, so that when it overcomes, coolness and moisture are weakened while heat and dryness prevail. But the weakened elements will be reinforced by a cold and moist body, which is water. In fact, the meaning of thirst is the need for what is cold and moist. And God the most high created the cold and the moist to assist coolness and moisture when they are overcome, and He created nourishment and medicines and other mutually opposing substances so that when something is overcome it may be countered by its opposite and be vanquished: this is what we mean by reinforcement. This is only accomplished by creating nourishment and medicines, creating the means to improve them, and the knowledge guiding us to using them. All of this is through God's—great and glorious—preserving the bodies of animals and composite things from conflicting elements.

These are the causes which preserve man from annihilation from within. But he is also subject to destruction from external causes, like dangerous predators and contentious enemies. He preserves man from that by creating spies to warn against the approach of the enemy—eyes and ears and others like them—which are his advance guard. Then He created a hand for him to strike with, and arms with which to repel, like armour and shields, as well as those with which to attack, like swords and knives. Then, should one be unable to repel them with these, He assists with means of flight: legs for ambulatory animals and wings for flying things. In similar fashion His preserving—may His power be exalted!—includes every atom in the kingdoms of heaven and of the earth, to the point where the core of the herbs which grow in the earth is preserved by a hard husk and its freshness is preserved by moisture. Furthermore, He preserves what is not protected by its husk alone with thorns growing from it [122] by which those animals harmful to it may be repelled. So thorns serve as arms for plants, much as horns, claws, and fangs serve for animals.

In fact, every drop of water has with it a protector to preserve it from the air which opposes it. For when water is placed in an open container and is left for a period of time, it is converted to air, and the air which opposes it robs it of the attribute of wetness. Yet if you dip a finger in water and then lift it up and invert it, a drop of water hangs from it, and it [the drop] stays inverted and does not detach itself, even though by nature it should fall to earth. For if it were to detach itself, small as it is, the air would overpower it and transform it. Rather it remains hanging there until the remaining moisture is gathered to it, so that the drop becomes bigger and it ventures to pass through the air quickly without the air overpowering it to transform it. This is not because the drop is preserving itself by knowing its weakness and the power of its opposite, as well as its need to borrow from the remaining moisture. It is rather preserved by an angel entrusted with it, who operates through an intention inhering in the essence of water. Indeed it is related in a report that not even a drop of rain falls without an angel with it to preserve it until it reaches its resting place on earth.[55] And that is true.

The interior vision of those who possess insight has already indicated it and guided us to it, for they believed the report not merely from traditional adherence but from insight into it. Moreover, a great deal can be said by way of explaining how God the most high preserves the heavens and the earth and what lies between them, as with the rest of His actions. And in that way this name will be known, not through knowing its derivation in language or by conjectures about the meaning of preserving in general. [123]

*Counsel*: The preserver among men is one who preserves his limbs and his heart; who preserves his life of faith from the assault of anger and the enticement of desire, self-deception and the delusion of Satan. Man is indeed 'at the brink of a bottomless precipice' surrounded by these perils which lead to perdition.

40. *Al-Muqīt*—the Nourisher—means the creator of nutriments and the one who delivers them to bodies as food, and to hearts as knowledge. It means the same as Provider [*al-Razzāq*], yet this name is more specific, since provision includes what is other than food as well as food', where food is what suffices to sustain the body.

Or it may mean the one who takes things over, the All-Powerful [cf. §69]. for taking over is achieved by power and knowledge. The saying of Him—great and glorious—indicates this: *And God is the nourisher of all things* (IV:85)—that is, cognizant and powerful, so that its meaning resolves to power and knowledge. We have already considered knowledge, and we shall consider power; yet concerning this meaning, describing it as the nourisher is more accurate than describing it as the powerful alone or the knower alone, for it signifies a combination of both, and so cannot be considered synonymous.

41. *Al-Ḥasīb*—the Reckoner—is the one who suffices, for He is all one needs who belongs to Him.[56] God—may He be praised and exalted—is the measurer of every single thing and the one who suffices for it. And it is inconceivable that this attribute, in its essential reality, be said of anything else, since for anything to be sufficient it must itself be all that it needs for its existence, the permanence of its existence, and the perfection of its existence. And there is nothing in existence which by itself suffices for anything, except God—great and glorious, for He alone suffices for everything, not for some things only. He alone suffices, that is, in that things attain existence from Him, and their existence perdures and is made perfect by Him. [124]

Do not imagine that when you need food, drink, earth, sky, sun, or the like, that you need something other than Him, or that He is not all you need. He is the one who supplies all you need by creating food and drink, heaven and earth, so He is all you need. Nor should you think that God is not the one who protects and suffices in the case of an infant who needs his mother to nurse him and care for him. Indeed, God—great and glorious—suffices for him, since He created his mother and the milk in her breasts, as well as the guidance needed for him to swallow it. He also created the tenderness and love in the heart of the mother, so that she [will] enable him to devour her milk, calling him to it and prompting him to do so. Now sufficiency is only attained by these means, and God the most high alone possesses the ability to create it for the infant. Should it be said to you that the mother alone is sufficient for the infant and that she is all he needs, you would believe that and not say: but she is hardly sufficient for him since he needs milk and how can a mother suffice for him when there is no milk? Rather you would say: indeed, he needs milk, but milk also comes from the mother, so he needs no-one else except the mother. But you should know that milk does not come from the mother, but together with the mother comes from God—may He be praised and exalted, and from His graciousness and generosity. For He alone is all that each thing needs; nothing [except He] exists which alone suffices for anything at all. Rather things depend on each other, while everything depends on the power of God—may He be praised and exalted.

*Counsel*: There is no access to this attribute for men except by way of a remote metaphor, or as part of a prevalent popular opinion which does not think twice about it. Metaphorically, it is like this: even if one were sufficient for his infant in sustaining his care, or sufficient for his student in educating him to the point where he is no longer in need of assistance from someone else, he would be but a means to sufficiency and not himself sufficient. For it is God—may He be praised and exalted—who suffices, and since man neither subsists by his own power nor is sufficient [125] unto himself, how can he suffice for another?

As part of a prevalent opinion, it is like this: even if one be deemed to be sufficient in himself and not as a means, nevertheless he is not alone sufficient since he needs, a place to receive his action and his sufficiency. Moreover, this is the least of the things at issue, for the heart which is the locus of knowledge is clearly necessary in the first place so that he may be sufficient in giving instruction. And the stomach which is the receptacle for food is needed to enable him to be sufficient[57] in conveying food to his body. All this, along with many other things one needs are beyond one's reckoning, nor do any of them fall under his free choice. For the lowest rank of action requires an agent and a recipient, and the agent will not suffice at all without a recipient. This is only fulfilled in God—great and glorious, since He creates the action as well as creating the place to receive it, the conditions pertaining to its reception and whatever surrounds it. Nevertheless, it may be that one would turn spontaneously and unreflectively to the agent, without considering the situation surrounding it, and deem the agent alone to be sufficient to the task, but such is not the case.[58]

Indeed, the religious fruit from this for a man is that God alone suffices for him, in connection with his intention and his will, so that he wants only God—great and glorious. He should not want paradise nor should his heart be preoccupied with hell, trying to be on guard against it, but his intention should be absorbed by God alone, the most high.[59] And if God reveals Himself in His majesty, he should say: this is sufficient for me, for I do not want anything other than Him nor do I care whether something other than Him escapes me or not. [126]

42. *Al-Jalīl*—the Majestic—is the one qualified by the attributes of majesty. Now the attributes of majesty are might, dominion, sanctification, knowledge, wealth, power, and other attributes we have mentioned. And the one who combines all of them is the absolutely majestic, while the majesty of one qualified by some of these attributes is proportional to what he receives of those particular attributes. So the absolutely majestic is none other than God—great and glorious. And as[60] 'the Great' refers to the perfection of essence, and 'the Majestic' to perfection of attributes, so does 'the Tremendous' refer to perfection of essence and attributes together, as perceived by intellectual insight—provided it encompasses the intellectual perception rather than being encompassed by it.

Moreover, when the attributes of majesty are related to the intellectual perception apprehending them, they are called beauty, and the one qualified by them is called beautiful. The term 'beautiful' was posited initially for the external form apprehended by sight, to the extent that it was adapted to sight and suited it, and later transferred to the interior form which is apprehended by insight, so that one could say: 'good and beautiful comportment' or 'beautiful disposition'—and that is perceived by insight rather than by sight. When an interior form is perfect, properly proportioned, and combines all of the perfection appropriate to it, as befits it and in the proper manner, then it is beautiful in relation to the interior insight apprehending it, and adapted to it in a way that whoever beholds it will experience far more pleasure, joy, and excitement than the observer who views the beautiful form with [127] external sight only. For the absolute and truly beautiful one is God alone—may He be praised and exalted—since all the beauty, perfection, splendour, and attractiveness in the world comes from the lights of His essence and the traces of His attributes. There is no existing thing in the world except Him which has absolute perfection with no competitor, be it actual or potential. For that reason the one who knows Him or contemplates His beauty experiences such delight, happiness, pleasure and joy that he disdains the delight of paradise as well as the beauty of sensible forms. Indeed, there is no comparison between the beauty of external forms and the beauty of interior meaning apprehended by intellectual perception.

We have removed the veil from this meaning in the 'Book of Love [Desire, Intimacy, and Acceptance]' (XXXVI) in the *Revival of the Religious Sciences*.[61] Once it is established that He is beautiful and majestic, then every beautiful thing will be loved and desired by whomsoever perceives its beauty. For that reason is God—great and glorious—loved by those who know Him, as external beautiful forms are loved by those who see, not by those who are blind.

*Counsel*: The majestic and beautiful among men is the one whose interior attributes are attractive so as to give pleasure to discerning hearts; exterior beauty is of lesser worth.

43. *Al-Karīm*—the Generous—is one who forgives if he has the power, follows through when he promises, and exceeds the limits one could hope for when he gives; nor is he concerned how much he gives or to whom he gives. If a need is brought before someone else, he is unhappy; if he is treated badly,

he reproves but does not pursue it. Whoever seeks refuge and support with him is not lost, and one may dispense with entreaties and mediators. Now the one who unites all this in himself, without affectation, is the absolutely generous one, and that belongs to God alone—may He be praised and exalted. [128]

*Counsel*: Man may endeavour to acquire these qualities, but only in some things and with a sort of affectation.[62] In this way he may be characterized as generous, yet he remains deficient by comparison with the absolutely generous. How can he not be so characterized when the messenger of God—may God's mercy and peace be upon him—said: 'Do not call the grapevine generous; it is the Muslim who is generous'.[63] Now it is said that the grapevine is described as generous because it is a compliant shrub, with delicious fruit that is easy to pick, within reach, and free from thorns and other causes of harm—unlike the date palm.

44. *Al-Raqīb*—the All-Observant—is one who knows and protects. For whoever cares for something to the point of never forgetting it, and observes it with a constant and persistent gaze—so that if one to whom it was forbidden knew about the surveillance he would not approach it: such a one is called observant. It is as though this name refers to knowledge and protection together, but with regard to its being constant and persistent, in addition to there being something forbidden and protected from access.

*Counsel*: The attribute of watchfulness is only praiseworthy in man if his watchfulness is directed to his Lord and his heart. And that will be the case when he knows that God the most high observes him and sees him in every situation, as well as knowing that his own soul is an enemy to him, and that Satan is his enemy; and that both of them take the opportunity to prompt him to forgetfulness and disobedience. So he becomes wary with regard to both of them by noticing their abode, their deceptions, and the occasions of their eruption, so that he can block both of them from using the entrances and the exits to his heart—that is his watchfulness. [129]

45. *Al-Mujīb*—the Answerer of prayers—is the one who responds to the requests of those who ask by assisting them, to the call of those who call upon him by answering them, and responds to the plight of the poor with all they need. In fact, he blesses before the request and grants favours before the entreaty. But that belongs to God alone—great and exalted, for He knows the needs of the needy before they [even] ask; indeed He already knew them in eternity, so He arranged the sources sufficient to their needs by creating food and nourishment, and by facilitating both the causes and the means of fulfilling all these needs.

*Counsel*: Man needs to be responsive first of all to his Lord, in whatever He commands or forbids him to do, and whatever He assigns to him or summons him to do. Then to His servants, in whatever God—great and glorious—bestowed on him by way of enabling him to do it; and in assisting every beggar in whatever they ask him, if he is able to do it; or with a kind response if he is unable to do so. For God—great and glorious—said: *Therefore the beggar drive not away* (XCIII:10), while the messenger of God—may God's blessing and peace be upon him—said: 'If I am invited to eat a sheep's trotter I will comply, and if a shank is presented to me I will accept it'.[64] Furthermore his presence at invited events and his acceptance of gifts, represents the utmost of deference and responsiveness on his part. How many contemptible and proud people deem themselves above accepting every gift and would not deign to be present in response to every invitation, but rather maintain their distinction and greatness without any concern for the feelings of the one extending the invitation, or whether he may be hurt on account of them. But such people have no part in the meaning of this name.

46. *Al-Wāsiʿ*—the Vast—derives from expansiveness, and expansiveness is sometimes linked to knowledge, when it extends to and comprehends a multitude of objects; and at other times it is linked to charity and widespread blessings, extending as far as possible to whatever they descend upon. So the absolutely vast is God—may He be praised and exalted—for if His knowledge be considered, the sea of things He knows has no shore; in fact the seas would be exhausted if they were ink for His words.[65] And if His beneficence and blessing be considered, there is no end to the things He can do. Moreover, every expansiveness, [130] however immense, comes up against limits, so the one which does not come up against limits is most deserving of the name of expansiveness. Now God—may He be praised and exalted—is the absolutely vast, for everything that is vast is confined by comparison with what is yet more vast, and for every expansiveness which comes up against limits, additions to it may still be conceived. Yet it is inconceivable for anything to be added to what is without limit or boundary.

*Counsel*: Expansiveness for man consists in his knowledge and his character. For if his knowledge is increased, he is vast in proportion to the extent of his knowledge; and if his character expands to the point that it is not confined by fear of poverty or the anger which accompanies envy, or the dominance of greed, or other attributes—then he is vast. Yet all of that has limits; only God the most high is truly vast.

47. *Al-Ḥakīm*—the Wise—is the one who possesses wisdom. Wisdom is equivalent to knowledge of superior things through the highest modes of knowing. But the most sublime thing of all is God—may He be praised. And we have seen that no-one

other than He can truly know Him. He is the truly wise because He knows the most sublime things by the most sublime modes of knowing. For the most sublime mode of knowledge is the eternal everlasting knowledge whose extinction is inconceivable, and which corresponds to other modes of knowing in a way that admits no doubt or concealment. Only the knowledge of God—may He be praised and exalted—is so qualified. Indeed, one who is proficient in the fine points of craftsmanship and has mastered them to become skilled in fabricating is called wise, yet perfection in that also belongs to God the most high alone, for He is the truly wise.

*Counsel*: Whoever knows all things without knowing God—great and glorious—is not worthy to be called wise, because he does not know the most sublime and highest of things. Wisdom is the most sublime mode of knowledge, and the sublimity of knowledge is proportioned to the sublimity of its object, and there is none more sublime than God—great and glorious. [131] Moreover, whoever knows God the most high is wise, even if his aptitude be deficient in the other conventional modes of knowledge, or his speech be slow or faltering in expounding them. Nonetheless, comparing man's wisdom to the wisdom of God most high is like comparing his knowledge to God's knowledge of His essence; and what a difference there is between the two modes of knowing, and so between the two forms of wisdom. Yet however remote it may be from God's, man's knowledge of God is nonetheless the most precious and most beneficial knowledge, and *whoever is given wisdom is given a great good* (II:269).

Indeed the discourse of one who knows God is different from that of others. Rarely does he concern himself with particulars; he rather speaks of matters universal in scope. Nor does he attend to temporal advantage, but concerns himself with whatever will benefit him in the world to come. Perhaps it is because all this is more evident to people than the wise man's situation regarding his knowledge of God—great and glorious—that they apply the term 'wisdom' to the likes of universal statements, and call the ones who utter them wise.

That is like the saying of the master of men [Muḥammad]—may the blessings of the merciful One and His peace be upon him: 'the beginning of wisdom is fear of God'.[66] Or his saying—may God's blessing and peace be upon him: 'The shrewd man is one who judges his soul and works for whatever comes after death, while the incompetent subordinates his soul to its passions and hopes in God'.[67] Or his saying—may blessings and peace be upon him: 'That which is little yet sufficient is better than a great deal which distracts'.[68] Or his saying—may God's blessing and peace be upon him: 'For one who becomes healthy in his body, safe in his surroundings with his daily food, it is as though the world in its totality belongs to him'.[69] Or his saying—may the best of blessings be granted him: 'Be godfearing [*wariʿ*] and you will be the most worshipful of people; be content and you will be the most grateful of [132] people'.[70] Or his saying: 'speech is responsible for misfortune'.[71] Or his saying: 'Part of the attractiveness of a man's Islam is to leave alone that which does not concern him'.[72] Or his saying: 'The happy man is one who is instructed by [the fate of] another'.[73] Or his saying: 'Silence is wisdom, but few accomplish it'.[74] Or his saying: 'Contentment is a wealth that will not be consumed'.[75] Or his saying: 'Perseverance is half of faith; certainty is the whole of faith'.[76] These expressions and their like are termed wisdom, and whoever is adept at them is called wise.

48. *Al-Wadūd*—the Loving-kind—is one who wishes all creatures well and accordingly favours them and praises them. Its meaning is close to 'the Merciful', but mercy is linked with one who receives mercy, and the one who receives mercy is needy and poor. So the actions of the Merciful presuppose there being one who is weak to receive mercy, while the actions

of the Loving-kind do not require that. Rather, bestowing favours from the outset results from loving-kindness. Just as the meaning of His mercy—may He be praised and exalted—consists in His intending the well-being of the one who receives mercy and in His giving him all that he needs, while He is free from the empathy usually associated with mercy, so does His loving-kindness consist in His intending honour and blessing and in His favour and grace, while He transcends the natural inclination usually associated with love and mercy. In fact, love and mercy are only intended for the benefit and advantage of those who receive mercy or are loved; they do not find their cause in the sensitiveness or natural inclination of the Loving kind One. For another's benefit is the heart and soul of mercy and love and that is how the case of God—may He be praised and exalted—is to be conceived: absent those features which human experience associates with mercy and love yet which do not contribute to the benefit they bring.

*Counsel*: One is loving-kind among God's servants who desires for God's creatures whatever he desires for himself; and whoever prefers them to himself is even higher than that. Like one of them who said: 'I would like to be a bridge over the fire [i.e., hell] so that creatures might pass over me and not be harmed by it'. The perfection of that virtue occurs when not even [133] anger, hatred, and the harm he might receive can keep him from altruism and goodness. As the messenger of God—may God's blessing and peace be upon him—said, when his tooth was broken and his face was struck and bloodied: 'Lord, guide my people, for they do not know'.[77] Not even their actions prevented him from intending their good. Or as he—may God's blessing and peace be upon him—commanded ʿAlī—may God be merciful to him—when he said: 'If you want to take precedence over those who are close to God, then be reconciled with those who broke with you, give to the ones who excluded you, and forgive the ones who wronged you'.[78]

49. *Al-Majīd*—the All-Glorious—is one who is noble in essence, beautiful in actions, and bountiful in gifts and in favours. It is as if nobility of essence is called 'glory' when goodness of action is combined with it. He is also the one who glorifies [*al-Majīd*]—yet one of these [glorious, glorifier] is more indicative of intensification. It is as if it [*al-Majīd*, the All-Glorious] combines the meanings of the Majestic [*al-Jalīl*], the Bestower [*al-Wahhāb*] and the Generous [*al-Karīm*]—and we have discussed them previously [cf. §§42, 17, 43].

50. *Al-Bāʿith*—the Raiser of the dead—is the one who gives creatures life on the day of resurrection, *raising up those in the grave* (XXII:7), and *revealing what is in men's hearts* (C:10). Raising of the dead is the final birth, and knowledge of this name is contingent upon a true knowledge of the resurrection, yet that is one of the most hidden forms of knowledge. Most creatures entertain common illusions and vague imaginings regarding it, the upshot of which is their imagining death to be mere non-existence, or that the resurrection brings forth something new in the wake of nothing, as in the first creation. Their belief that death is non-existence is mistaken, as is their opinion that the second creation is like the first one. [134]

Concerning their belief that death is non-existence, it is groundless. 'Indeed, the grave is either one of the pits of the fires of hell or one of the gardens of paradise'.[79] So the dead are either happy—and these are not *dead, nay they are living. With their Lord they have provision. Jubilant* [*are they*] *because of what God hath bestowed on them of His bounty* (III:169-70), or they are wretched, yet these too are alive. That was the reason why the Messenger of God—may God's blessing and peace be upon him—addressed them in the battle of Badr, when he said: 'I have found what my Lord promised me to be true; have you found what your Lord promised to be true?' Then when it was said to him: 'How do you address people already cadaverous?' he responded: 'You are no better than they at hearing what I say; it is just that they cannot answer'.[80] Interior vision has guided the masters of intellectual perception to the fact that man was created for eternity and that there is no way for him to become non-existent. Of course, at one moment his behaviour may be separated from the body, and it is said: 'he is dead'; or again it may return to it, and it is said: 'he has come to life and is resurrected'—that is, his body has come to life. But this book cannot undertake to explore the depths of all that.

Now, concerning their opinion that the resurrection is not a second creation but is like the first coming-to-be, that is not sound, for the resurrection is another sort of creation [*inshā'*] quite unrelated to the first. Indeed, there are many comings-to-be proper to man, and not simply two of them. And for that reason the most high said: *That we may transfigure you and make you what you know not* (LVI:61). And in the same way He said after creating the little lump, the clot, and the rest: *then* [*We*] *produced it as another creation. So blessed be God, the Best of Creators*! (XXIII:14) Indeed, sperm originates from the earth, the clot from sperm, the lump from the clot, [135] and the spirit from the lump. It was in response to the exalted origin of the spirit, to its glory, and to its being a divine thing, that He said: '*then* [*We*] *produced it as another creation. So blessed be God the best creators*!' (XXIII:14) And the most high said: *They will ask thee concerning the Spirit. Say: the Spirit is by command of my Lord* (XVII:85).[81] So the creation of sensory perceptions after creating the spiritual foundation is another creation, while the creation of discernment which appears after seven years is yet another creation, and the creation of reason after fifteen years (or thereabouts) is a further creation. So each origination is a stage, so *he created you by* [divers] *stages* (LXXI:14). Furthermore, the appearance of the characteristic of holiness [*wilāya*] in the ones endowed with this quality is another creation, while the appearance of prophethood after that is yet another, indeed it is a kind of resurrection. So God—may He be praised and exalted—is the one who raises [*bāʿith*] up the messengers, as He is the one who will raise us all up on the day of resurrection.

Just as a true understanding of discernment is difficult for an infant before it has attained the level of discernment, and a true understanding of reason and of the wonders revealed in this stage is difficult before attaining to the level of reason, in a similar way understanding the stage of holiness and prophecy is difficult during the stage of reason. For holiness is a stage of perfection that comes after the creation of reason, as reason is a stage of perfection after the creation of discernment, and discernment is a stage after the creation of the senses. Similarly, it is a part of human nature for men to deny what they have not achieved or attained, to the point where each person tends to deny what he does not see or what he has not attained rather than believe what is hidden from him. So it is natural to them to deny [136] holiness and its wonders as well as prophecy with its hidden secrets; indeed it is characteristic of them to deny the second creation and the next life, since they have not yet attained it. And if the stage of reason, with its universe and the wonders manifest to it were set forth before one who had only attained to the stage of discernment, he would deny it all, renouncing it and disclaiming its very existence. Yet whoever believes in something to which he has not attained believes in what he cannot see [*al-ghayb*], and that is the key to happiness.

Just as the stage of reason, with its perceptions and what comes to be with it can hardly be compared with the perceptions which preceded it, so it is with the next creation, yet even more so. One ought not to make comparisons between the next creation and the first. These creations are stages of a single essence and the steps by which it ascends to the stages of perfection, until it edges closer to the presence which is the utmost of all perfection, and that is to be with God—great and glorious: suspended between rejection and acceptance, separation and attainment. If one is accepted, he is raised to the highest of heights; otherwise he is banished to the lowest depths. What the present point intends is that there is no relation between the two creations except in name. So whoever does not know the creation and the resurrection will not know the meaning of the name 'The Raiser of the dead'. But that explanation would be quite extended, so we shall leave it behind.

*Counsel*: The truth of the resurrection refers to bringing the dead to life by creating them once more. Ignorance is the greatest death and knowledge the noblest life. God—may He be praised and exalted—mentioned knowledge and ignorance in His holy book, and called them life and death. Whoever lifts another out of ignorance to knowledge has already created him anew and revivified him to a blessed life. And should a man have a way of conveying knowledge to people and calling them to the Most High that would be a kind of revivification, and such would be the level of prophets and the scholars who are their heirs. [137]

51. *Al-Shahīd*—the Universal Witness—refers in its meaning to knowledge with a specific addition, for God—great and glorious—is *knower of invisible as well as visible things* (IX:94). Now the invisible [*ghayb*] comprises whatever is interior and the visible [*shahāda*] whatever is external, and this is what is seen. So if one considers knowledge alone, He is the one who knows [§20], while if it is linked to invisible and interior things, He is the One who is aware of everything [§32]; and if it be linked to external things, He is the Universal Witness. And it may be considered as well that He will bear witness to mankind on the day of resurrection from what He knows and has seen concerning them. The explication of this name is close to the explication of the Omniscient [§20] and the One who is aware of everything [§32], so we shall not repeat it.

52. *Al-Ḥaqq*—the Truth—is the one who is the antithesis of falsehood, as things may become evident by their opposites. Now everything of which one is aware may be absolutely false, absolutely true, or true in one respect and false in another. Whatever is impossible in itself is absolutely false, while that which is necessary in itself is absolutely true, and whatever is possible in itself and necessary by another is true in one respect and false in another. For this last has no existence in itself and so is false, yet acquires existence from the side of what is other than it, so it is an existent in this respect that acquired existence is bestowed upon it—so in that respect it is true while from the side of itself it is false.[82] For that reason the Most High said: *everything is perishing but His face* (XXVIII:88). He is forever and eternally thus; not in one state to the exclusion of another, for everything besides Him—forever and eternally—is not deserving of existence with respect to its own essence but only deserves it by virtue of Him, for in itself it is false; it is true only in virtue of what is other than it. From this you will know that the absolutely true is the One truly existing in itself, from which every true thing gets its true reality. [138]

It may also be said about the judgment, by which reason asserts that something exists, that it is true in the measure that it corresponds to the thing. Considered in itself, the judgment may be said to exist, but considered in relation to the reason which understands it in its intentional role, it is said to be true. Therefore, the existent most deserving of being called true is God the most high, and the knowledge which most deserves to be called true is the knowledge of God—great and glorious—for it is true in itself: that is, it corresponds to what is known, forever and eternally. Moreover, it corresponds through itself and not through something else; not like knowledge derived from another existing thing, for that obtains only so long as the other exists, and should it become nothing, the belief about it will be false. So that belief as well is not true by virtue of the essence of the thing believed, since that very thing does not exist by virtue of itself but by virtue of another.

And this may also be applied to assertions, as one speaks of a true or false assertion. And so far as that is concerned, the most true assertion is your saying: there is no god but God, for it is correct forever and eternally, by virtue of itself and not by virtue of another.

Therefore, 'true' applies to existence in individuals, to existence in the intellect, which is knowledge; and to existence in speech, which is utterance. The thing which most deserves to be [called] true is the one whose existence is established by virtue of its own essence, forever and eternally, and its knowledge as well as the witness to it is true forever and eternally. So all that pertains to the essence of the truly existing One, and to nothing else. [139]

*Counsel*: Man's share in this name lies in seeing himself as false, and not seeing anything other than God—great and glorious—as true. For if a man is true, he is not true in himself but true in God—great and glorious, for he exists by virtue of Him and not in himself; indeed he would be nothing had the Truth not created him. So the one who said: 'I am the truth'[83] was wrong, unless it be taken according to one of two interpretations, the first of which being that he means he exists by virtue of the Truth. But this interpretation is far-fetched because the statement does not communicate it, and because that would hardly be proper only to him, since everything besides the Truth exists by virtue of the Truth.

On the second interpretation, he is so absorbed in the Truth that he has no room for anything else. One may say of what takes over the totality of a thing and absorbs it that one *is* it, as the poet says: 'I am whom I desire, and he whom I desire is I', and by that he means that he is absorbed in it [*istighrāq*]. Among Sufi groups the name of God the most high which most often flows from their lips in their statements and during states of prayer is *al-Ḥaqq* [the Truth], in the measure that they attain to experience of self-annihilation with regard to their own essence, for they see the truly real essence to the exclusion of that which in itself is perishing. As for the practitioners of *Kalām*, the name which flows most frequently from their lips is *al-Bārī'* [the Producer], which has the same meaning as *al-Khāliq* [the Creator], since they are still at the level of reasoning to God by way of His actions. Most men see everything but Him, so they cite what they see as witness for Him, and these are the ones addressed by the saying of the most High: *Have they not considered the dominion of the heavens and the earth, and what things God has created?* (VII:185) Yet the righteous [*ṣiddīqūn*] do not see anything but Him, so they cite Him as witness for Himself, and so they are the ones addressed by the saying of the most High: *Does not thy Lord suffice, since He is Witness over all things* (XLI:53)?[84] [140]

53. *Al-Wakīl*—the Trustee—is one who has matters entrusted to him. But those so entrusted may be distinguished into one entrusted with some things (and that one is deficient) or one to whom everything is entrusted, and this is none but God—may He be praised and exalted. Again, those entrusted may be distinguished into one who deserves to be entrusted with something, not by nature but by empowerment and delegation (yet such a one is deficient in that he needs the empowerment and delegation); or one who by his very nature deserves to have matters entrusted to him and in whom hearts place their trust, not by appointment or empowerment on the part of someone else—and that is the absolute Trustee. Again, trustees may be distinguished into those who carry out whatever is entrusted to them perfectly with no shortcomings, or those who do not fulfil everything. Yet the absolute trustee is one to whom things are entrusted, who is fully capable of carrying them out, and faithful in executing them perfectly. That is none other than God the most high. So you should now understand the extent to which men may enter into the meaning of this name.

54–55. *Al-Qawī, Al-Matīn*—the Strong, the Firm. Strength indicates perfect power, while firmness indicates intensification of strength. So God—may He be praised and exalted, insofar as He possesses the utmost power and is perfect in it, is the strong one; and in so far as He has intense strength, He is firm. This comes down to the meaning of strength, which will be treated later [§69].

56. *Al-Walī*—the Patron—is lover and protector. We have already treated the meaning of His love and affection [§48], and the meaning of His protection is evident, in that He suppresses the enemies of religion and supports its friends. God—may He be praised and exalted—said: *God is the patron of those who believe* (II:257). The Most High also said: *That is because God is patron of those who believe, and because the disbelievers have no patron* (XLVII:11). That is, He is not their protector. For He said—the great and glorious: *God has decreed: Lo! I verily shall conquer, I and my messengers* (LVIII:21). [141]

*Counsel*: Among men a patron is one who loves God—great and glorious—and loves His friends, who helps Him and helps His friends, and shows enmity towards His enemies. And among His enemies are one's own self and Satan, so that whoever forsakes these two and thereby promotes the affairs of God most high, befriending His friends and showing enmity to His enemies, is a patron among men.

57. *Al-Ḥamīd*—the Praised—is the one who is praised and extolled. God—great and glorious—is the Praised by virtue of His praise of Himself from eternity, and by virtue of His servants' praise for Him forever. But this comes down to the attributes of majesty [cf. §42], of exaltation [cf. §37], and of perfection, as they are linked to the repetition of those who continuously remember Him, for praise involves recalling the attributes of perfection insofar as they are perfect.[85]

*Counsel*: The one praised among men is the one whose beliefs, character, and actions are all praised without any contender, and that is Muḥammad—may God's blessing and peace be upon him, as well as whoever comes close to him among the prophets, and the others among the saints and scholars. Each one of them is praised in the measure that his faith, character, actions or assertions are praised. Yet since no one is free from blame or deficiency, though his praiseworthy attributes may be many, the only one praised absolutely is God the most high.

58. *Al-Muḥṣī*—the Knower of each separate thing—is the one who knows, yet when knowledge is linked to the objects known, insofar as it enumerates the objects, counts them, and so comprehends them, it is called reckoning [*iḥṣā'*]. The one who knows each separate thing absolutely is the one in whose knowledge the limits of each object as well as its quantity and dimensions are revealed. [142]

So far as man is concerned, although it is possible for him to reckon some objects by his knowledge, it is unable to circumscribe most of them. So his access to this name is tenuous, much like his access to the principles of knowledge.

59-60. *Al-Mubdi*ᶜ, *Al-Mu*ᶜ*īd*—the Beginner, the Restorer—mean the one who bestows existence [*mūjid*], but when this origination is not preceded by something like it, it is called a beginning; and when it is preceded by something like it, it is called a restoration. Now God—may He be praised and exalted—initiated the creation of mankind and He is also the one who will restore them, that is, gather them together on the day of resurrection. For all things began for Him and are restored to Him; began in Him and in Him are restored.

61-62. *Al-Muḥyī, Al-Mumīt*—the Life-Giver, the Slayer—this also comes down to bringing into existence, but when the object is life, making it is called animation, while if the object is death, doing it is called killing. None is the creator of death and of life but God—may He be praised and exalted, and so there is no life-giver or slayer but God—great and glorious. Some indications of the meaning of 'life' were already given in treating the name *al-Bāʿith* [the Raiser of the dead—§50], so we shall not add to it.

63. *Al-Ḥayy*—the Living—is both agent and perceiver, so much so that one who does not act or perceive at all is dead. The lowest level of perception involves the one perceiving being conscious of itself, for what is not conscious of itself is inanimate and dead. But the perfect and absolute living thing is one under whose perception all perceived things are arranged, as are all existing things under its activity, so that no perceived thing escapes its knowledge and no action its activity, and that is God—great and glorious, for He is the absolutely living one. As for every living thing other than He, its life is commensurate with its perception and its activity, and all of that is circumscribed within narrow limits. Furthermore, the living things diverge among themselves in this, and their ranking is a function of this divergence, as we indicated earlier in considering the ranks of angels, men, and beasts. [143]

64. *Al-Qayyūm*—the Self-Existing. You must know that things are distinguished into what requires a subject, like accidents and attributes, of which it is said that they do not subsist in themselves; and into what does not need a subject, of which it is said that it subsists in itself, like substances. Yet while a substance may have no need of a substratum in which to subsist, given that it subsists in itself, it nevertheless remains in need of things necessary for its existence, and they are conditions for its existing. So it is not really subsistent in itself, since it requires the existence of another to subsist, even if it does not need a substratum [or subject, in which to subsist].[86]

If an existent were to exist whose essence would suffice for itself, whose subsistence would not be from another, and whose existence would not be conditioned by the existence of another, it would subsist in itself absolutely. If beyond that, every existent subsisted by virtue of it, such that the existence and conservation of things would be inconceivable without it, that would be the self-existing one since it subsisted in itself and each thing subsisted by it. But that is none other than God—may He be praised and exalted. And man's access to this attribute is in proportion to his detachment from everything that is not God the most high.

65. *Al-Wājid*—the Resourceful—is one who lacks nothing: the very opposite of one in need. Someone who lacks what is not necessary for him to exist would probably not be called needy, nor would someone who possessed what is essentially irrelevant to him and fails to contribute to his perfection be called resourceful. Rather, the resourceful one is he who does not lack anything necessary to him, and everything necessary in the attributes of divinity and their perfection is present in God—may He be praised and exalted. So He is resourceful by this consideration; in fact, He is absolutely resourceful. But anyone besides Him, even though he be endowed with a few of the attributes of perfection as well as their causes, will still lack many others, and so can only be said to be resourceful, relatively speaking. [144]

66. *Al-Mājid*—the Magnificent—means the same as *al-Majīd* [the All-Glorious, §49], just as the knower [*ʿalīm*] means the same as the knowing one [*ʿālim*]. In fact, the paradigm *fāʿil* is even more emphatic, and we have already treated its meanings.

67. *Al-Wāḥid*—the Unique—is the one who can neither be divided nor duplicated. Concerning its not being divisible, it is like a unitary substance which cannot be divided: it is said

to be one in the sense that no part of it is itself a substance, as a point has no parts. And God the most high is one in the sense that it is impossible for His essence to be arranged into parts.

Concerning its not being able to be duplicated, that reflects its having no equal, like the sun. For while it is subject to division in imagination and is divisible in its essence because it is a kind of body, nevertheless it has no equal, even though it is possible for it to have one. So if there actually were an existent so individuated by the existence proper to it that it was inconceivable for another to share in it at all, that one would be absolutely one, eternally and forever. A man may be unique when he has no equal among his fellow men in a characteristic reckoned among good qualities, yet that is a function of the class of men and the times, since it is possible that one like him emerge in another time, and furthermore, it is said in relation to some qualities and not all. So it belongs to none but God to be absolute unity.

68. *Al-Ṣamad*—the Eternal—is the one to whom one turns in need and the one who is intended in our desires, for ultimate dominion culminates in him. The one whom God has appointed to be a model for His servants in fulfilling their worldly and religious duties, and who secures the needs of His creatures by his word and action—to that one God bestows a share in this attribute.[87] But the absolutely eternal is the one to whom one turns in every need, and He is God—may He be praised and exalted. [145]

69-70. *Al-Qādir, Al-Muqtadir*—the All-Powerful, the All-Determiner—both mean 'one who possesses power', but 'the All-Determiner' is more emphatic. Power is equivalent to the intention by which a thing comes into existence according to a determinate plan of will and knowledge, and in conformity with both of them. The All-Powerful is one who does what he wills, or does not act if he so wills, and is not so conditioned as to will necessarily. So God is all-powerful in that He could bring about the resurrection now, and He would bring it about were He to will it. So if He does not bring it about, that is because He has not willed it, and He does not will it to happen now inasmuch as His knowledge had previously fixed its appointed time and moment according to plan, which hardly detracts from His power. The absolutely powerful is He who creates each existent individually without needing assistance from anyone else, and this is God most high.

So far as man is concerned, he is possessed of power in a general sense but deficiently so, for he only attains some possibilities. It is not within his power to create, yet God the most high is Himself creator of human powers by His power, inasmuch as He puts all the existing causes at the service of man's power. But a book like this one is not able to probe below this depth.

71-72. *Al-Muqaddim, Al-Mu'akhkhir*—the Promoter, the Postponer—is the one who brings close and who pushes away, and whomever he brings close he promotes, while those whom he pushes away he banishes. So He promotes His prophets and friends by bringing them close to Him and guiding them, while He banishes His enemies by pushing them away and putting a barrier between Himself and them. So, for example, when a king brings two persons close to him, but places one of them closer to himself, he is said to have promoted him by giving him precedence over the other.

Precedence can sometimes be in position and sometimes in rank, and is inevitably related to something which comes behind it. And just as inevitably there is something intended—the goal—in relation to which whatever is promoted is promoted, and what is set back is set back. Now the one intended is God—may He be praised and exalted, and the one promoted with respect to God most high [146] is the one brought close to Him [*muqarrab*]. Thus He has promoted, in order, angels, prophets, friends, and scholars. Whoever is set back is behind with respect to those ahead of him but ahead of those behind him. And God—may He be praised and exalted—is the one who promotes and sets back. For if you attribute their promotion or setback to their own industry or shortcomings, or to their excellence or deficiency in attributes, then who is it who has prompted them to industry by promoting their knowledge, or to worship by stimulating their motives? Similarly, who is it who prompted them to fall short by altering their motives into the very opposite of the straight path? But all of this comes from God most high, for He is the Promoter and the Postponer: what He intends is promotion or demotion in rank, which should indicate that whoever is promoted has not been promoted by virtue of his knowledge or action, but by the promotion of God—great and glorious—Himself. And similarly for the one set back. As the saying of the Most High states explicitly: *Lo, those unto whom kindness hath gone forth before Us, they will be far removed from thence* (XXI:101). And the Most High again: *And if We had so willed, We could have given every soul guidance, but the word from Me concerning evildoers took effect:* [*that I will fill*] *hell* [*with the jinn and mankind together*] (XXXII:13)—and the verse continues.

*Counsel*: Man's share in these attributes of actions is obvious, so we will not occupy ourselves with reiterating it for every name, for fear of prolixity. And besides, from what we have mentioned concerning it, you should know how to complete it.

73-74. *Al-Awwal, Al-Ākhir*—the First, the Last. You should know that whatever is first is first with respect to something, and what is last is so with respect to something, and that they are opposites. For it is inconceivable that there be one thing which is first and last at once, in a single respect and in relation to the same thing. Yet when you ponder the order of existence and consider the ordered chain of beings, God [147] the most high is first with respect to it, since all of them receive their existence from Him, and He does not receive existence from another but is existent by His essence.

Whenever you ponder the order of wayfaring and observe the stages attained by those journeying towards Him, He is the last, for He is the final point to which the levels of 'knowers' ascend.[88] For every knowing experienced this side of knowledge of Him is a step towards knowledge of Him. The highest stage is knowledge of God—may He be praised and exalted. So He is last with respect to wayfaring, and first with respect to existence: the first beginning was from Him; and to Him is the last return and destination.

75-76. *Al-Ẓāhir, Al-Bāṭin*—the Manifest, the Hidden—these two attributes are also to be taken relatively, for what is manifest can be evident to one thing and hidden from another. Yet it cannot be manifest and hidden in one and the same respect; though it may be manifest in relation to a perception and hidden in another respect. For things are manifest or hidden only in relation to modes of perception. Now God—may He be praised and exalted—is hidden when He is sought by sensory perception or using the resources of imagination, yet manifest when sought by way of inference using the resources of reason. But if you say: so far as His being hidden with respect to sensory perception, that is evident; but as to His being manifest to reason, that is obscure, since what is manifest is that which is not in doubt and about whose perception men do not differ; yet this subject is one over which much doubt arises among men, so how can it be evident? But you should realize that He is hidden in His manifestations by the intense way in which He is manifest, for His manifestness is the reason for His being hidden, as His very light blocks His light. So it is that whatever broaches its limits is turned into its opposite.

Perhaps you are astonished by this teaching, and find it far-fetched, so you may need an example to understand it. [148] So I say: if you considered a single word written by an Author, you would infer from it that an Author exists who is knowledgeable, competent, able to hear and see; and you would derive from that the certainty that those attributes exist. Furthermore, if you saw a written word, that would lead you to a definite certainty regarding the existence of its Author—knowledgeable, competent, able to hear and see, and living—but nothing points to him except the shape of a single word. Yet just as your seeing this word offers clear testimony to the attributes of the Author, so there is not an atom in the heavens and the earth, no planet, star, sun or moon, animal or plant, or characteristic of any subject, which does not bear witness by itself to the need for an organizer to arrange it, plan it, and specify it with its proper qualities. Nor can man consider himself, in the arrangement of his members and parts among themselves, external and internal, as well as the attributes and states of his which carry on autonomically through no choice of his, without seeing in them an eloquent witness to the one who created them, determined them and arranged them. So it is with everything that sees with all its senses, within itself or outside itself.

While things may differ in bearing witness, as some of them do while others do not, nevertheless certitude is attained overall. However, many witnesses, to the extent that they coincide, may be hidden or obscure due to the very intensity of their evidence. For instance, what is most evident is what is perceived by the senses, and the most evident of these is what is perceived by the sense of sight, and the most evident of the things perceived by the sense of sight is the light of the sun shining on bodies, by which everything becomes manifest. Now how can that by which everything becomes manifest not itself be manifest?

Yet that poses difficulties for many people, so that they say: coloured things have only their colours in them—like black or red, and do not have along with the colour a radiance [149] or a light connected with the colour. Yet these people are made conscious of light in coloured things by the contrast which they perceive between the shade and the positing of the light, as between night and day. For the sun may be thought to be hidden at night or eclipsed by dark objects during the day so that its effects are cut off from coloured things, so a contrast is noted between what is effected and illuminated by it and what is dark and shielded from it. So the existence of light is known by the absence of light, if the condition of absence is set beside the condition of existence; the contrast is perceived despite the fact that the colours perdure in both states. So if the light of the sun were to encompass every body visible to a person, and the sun were never hidden so that the contrast could be perceived, it would be impossible for one to know that light is an existing thing added to the colours, despite the fact that it is the most manifest of things, as that by which all things become visible.

Were it conceivable that God—the most high and holy One—cease to exist or be hidden from some things, heaven and earth would collapse along with everything cut off from His light, and the contrast between the two states would be perceived, and His existence would certainly become known! However, in as much as all things concur in bearing witness, and all the states succeed one another in a uniform order, this becomes the very cause of His being hidden. So Praise be to Him who is concealed from creatures by His light and hidden from them by the intensity of His manifestations: He is the manifest One than whom there is none more manifest, as well as the hidden One than whom none is more hidden.

*Counsel*: You must not marvel at this [apparent paradox] among the attributes of God—the most high and holy One, for the intention [i.e., *ratio*] by which a man is human is both manifest and hidden. It is manifest in that it may be inferred from his wise and orderly actions; hidden if it is sought by sensory perception. For the senses only bear [150] on the external skin, yet a man is not human by virtue of his visible skin. For if that skin were to be altered or even the rest of his parts changed, he would remain himself while his parts were changed. It could be that all the parts of a man after he has grown up are no longer the parts which were his when he was small. For they disintegrated over a long period of time, and were changed into one like them as a result of nourishment received, and yet his nature is not changed. For that nature is hidden from the senses, but manifest to reason by way of inferring to it from its results and its actions.

[77. *Al-Wālī*—the Ruler, 78. *Al-Mutaʿālī*—the Exalted, occur in Ghazālī's commentary after §85.]

79. *Al-Barr*—the Doer of Good—is the beneficent one [*muḥsin*]. The absolute doer of good is the one from whom every good deed and beneficence comes. Man can be a doer of good only in the measure that he keeps himself occupied with doing good, especially towards his parents, teachers, and elders. It is told of Moses—peace be upon him—that while his Lord was speaking to him he saw a man standing by the leg of the throne, and he marvelled at his exalted position, so he said: 'O Lord, how has this man attained this place?' And the Lord said: 'He was not envious of any of my servants for what I gave to them, and he was good to his parents'.[89] This is what it is to be a doer of good among men. Regarding the particulars of God the most high's doing good and His beneficence to His creatures, however, expounding it would be too long, and some of the things we have mentioned should inform one about it.

80. *Al-Tawwāb*—the Ever-Relenting—makes reference to facilitating the causes of repentance in His servants time and again by making manifest to them some of His signs,

conveying His counsel to them, and disclosing His deterrents and warnings to them—to the point where, once informed by His instruction of the dangers of their sins, they will begin to experience [151] the fear occasioned by His deterrents and have recourse to repentance, so that the favour of God the most high will return to them on His accepting [their turning to Him].

*Counsel*: Whoever accepts time and again the excuses of those who do wrong among those entrusted to his care, as well as those of his friends and acquaintances, is indeed characterized by this quality and has gained a share of it.

81. *Al-Muntaqim*—the Avenger—is the one who breaks the back of the recalcitrant, punishes criminals, and intensifies the punishment of the oppressor—but only after excusing and warning them, and after giving them the opportunity and the time to change. Yet this is harsher vengeance than a quick punishment, for when the punishment is swift, one does not persist in disobedience, and as a consequence he does not deserve the full punishment.

*Counsel*: Human vengeance is praiseworthy if it takes vengeance on the enemies of God the most high, and the worst such enemy is one's own lower soul. So it behooves him to take vengeance on it in as much as it yields to disobedience or fails in its duty of worship. As it is reported regarding Abū Yazīd—may God be merciful to him—that he said: 'My soul was so lazy one night as to keep me from a litany, so I punished it by depriving it of water for a year'.[90] In this way should one pursue the path of vengeance.

82. *Al-ʿAfū*—the Effacer of Sins—is the one who erases sins and overlooks acts of disobedience, and its meaning is close to *al-Ghafūr* [the All-Forgiving, §35]; except that this name is more

expressive than that, for 'all-forgiving' connotes concealment, while 'effacer' suggests erasing, and erasing is more effectual than concealment.

Man's share in this name should be clear: he is one who excuses [*ᶜafw*] everyone who harms him, doing good for him instead, as he sees God the most high doing good in this world to the disobedient and the unbeliever rather than bringing them swiftly to punishment. And he may excuse them by relenting towards them, for should [152] he thus relent, their sins will be erased, since 'the one who repents of wrongdoing becomes like one who did no wrong',[91] and this is the utmost point of erasing the crime.

83. *Al-Ra'ūf*—the All-Pitying—is one who possesses pity, and pity is an intensification of mercy. So its meaning is the same as 'the Merciful' [§3], although more emphatic, and we have already explained it.

84. *Mālik al-Mulk*—the King of Absolute Sovereignty—is the one who carries out what he wills in his kingdom, in the manner that he wills and as he wills it, bringing into being and destroying, perpetuating and annihilating. *Al-Mulk* here means 'kingdom', and *al-Mālik* means the powerful one with perfect power. All existent things form a single kingdom, and He is their king and the one holding power over them. All existent things form one kingdom only because they are connected one with another, so even if they are many in one respect, they are one in another. This is much like the human body, which is like a kingdom for the essence of man: many different members cooperating, as it were, in realizing the goal of one manager, and so forming a single kingdom. In that way, the entire world is like one person, with the parts of the world like his members, cooperating towards one goal, and its existence represents the highest possible realization of the good, as divine generosity requires.[92] Because its parts are arranged

in an orderly ranking and linked together by a single bond, they form one kingdom with God the most high as its sole king.

The kingdom of each man is his own body. For if what he wills is accomplished in the qualities of his heart and in his limbs, then he is king of the kingdom of himself according to the measure of power given to him.[93]

85. *Dhu'l-Jalāl wa'l-Ikrām*—the Lord of Majesty and Generosity—is the one from whom there is no majesty or perfection but that it is his, nor is there generosity or noble gift but that it flows from him. For majesty is His by nature while generosity emanates from Him [153] to His creation. And the various forms of generosity to His creation are hardly restricted or limited, as the saying of the Most High indicates: *verily We have honoured the children of Adam* (XVII:70).

77. *Al-Wālī*—the Ruler—is the one who plans the affairs of creation and rules them, that is, takes charge of them and so is fully charged with governing them. It is as though governing gives the sense of organization, power, and action, and the name 'ruler' cannot be used of whatever does not combine all of these in itself. So there is no ruler over things except God—may He be praised and exalted, for He is first of all their sole planner; secondly, the one who implements the plan by realizing it; and thirdly, the one who protects them by perpetuating and preserving them.

78. *Al-Mutaʿālī*—the Exalted—means the same as *Al-ʿAlī* [the High, §37], although its form is intensified; and that meaning has already been treated.

86. *Al-Muqsiṭ*—the Equitable—is he who demands justice for the wronged from the wrongdoer. Its perfection lies in linking the satisfaction of the wrongdoer [resulting from the crime] to the satisfaction of the one wronged, for that is the

ultimate in justice and equity, yet none is capable of it but God—may He be praised and exalted.

An example of this may be found in what is related of the Prophet—may God's blessing and peace be upon him—that once while he was seated he laughed so that his teeth showed, and ʿUmar—may God be pleased with him—said: 'My father and my mother be your ransom, O Messenger of God: what is it that made you laugh?' He said: 'Two men from my community fell on their knees before the Lord of Power, and one of them said: "O Lord, let this one make restitution to me for the way he has wronged me". And God—great and glorious—said: "Make restitution to your brother for the wrong you did to him". And he said: "O Lord, I have no good deeds left". So He said—the great and glorious One—to the petitioner: "How will you manage [154] with your brother since he has no good deeds left?" And that one said: "O Lord, let him relieve me of some of my burden of sin".' Then the Messenger of God began to weep—may God's blessing and peace be upon his tearful person—and said: 'What a mighty day that will be, when people will need others to relieve them of their burdens!' He went on to say: 'So God—great and glorious—said to the one who had been wronged: "Lift your eyes and look into paradise". And he said: "O Lord, I see cities of silver and palaces of gold decorated with pearls. For which prophet, righteous one, or martyr is this?" The Lord—great and glorious—said: "This belongs to whomever pays the price". And he said "O Lord, who can come up with such a sum?" But He said: "It is in your power". "But how, O Lord?" And He answered: "By forgiving your brother". And he said: "O Lord, I have already forgiven him". So God—great and glorious—said: "Take your brother by the hand and lead him into paradise".' Then the Prophet said—may God's blessing and peace be upon him: 'Fear God and make peace among yourselves, for God—may He be blessed and exalted—will make peace among the faithful on the day of resurrection'.[94]

This is the way of demanding and of granting justice, but no one is capable of acting like this but the Lord of Lords. Yet those men who have the greatest share in this name are those who insist first of all on justice from themselves for others, and then from one for another, but forbear demanding it from another for themselves.

87. *Al-Jāmiʿ*—the Uniter—is the one who combines similar things, dissimilar things, and opposites. So far as God's uniting similar things is concerned, one example would be His bringing many human beings together on the face of the earth; and another His gathering the distinguished among them on the plain of the resurrection. So far as dissimilar things are concerned, an example would be His uniting heavens, [155] stars, air, earth, sea, animals, plants, and diverse minerals. All of these have different shapes, colours, tastes, and properties, yet He has brought some of them together on earth, and has united all of them in the universe. In a similar way He has united bone, sinew, veins, muscles, brains, skin and blood, and the rest of the constituents of the humours in the body of animals. As for opposites, an example would be uniting heat with cold, and dry with wet in the physical constitution of animals, when these are incompatible with and resistant to each other. That is the most expressive aspect of uniting. One will only come to know the particulars of His uniting if one knows the particulars of the things He has united in this world and the next, and all that would take a long time to explain.

*Counsel*: Among men the one who unites is one who integrates the external behavior of his limbs with the inner realities of his heart. The one who unites is one in whom knowledge is perfect and behaviour admirable. So it is said: one is perfect when the light of his knowledge does not extinguish the light of his piety. For uniting steadfastness with insight is difficult, so you will see some steadfast in piety and asceticism yet lacking insight, or you will find some endowed with insight yet lacking steadfastness. So whoever unites steadfastness with insight will be known as one who unites. Enough!

88-89. *Al-Ghanī, Al-Mughnī*—the Rich, the Enricher. The rich one is he who has no connection with another—neither for his being nor for the attributes of his being, but rather transcends connections with things other than himself. For when one's being or the attributes of one's being depend on things outside oneself, then his existence and his perfection depend on them essentially, and he is actually poor: in need of acquiring what is his. Yet it is inconceivable that any but God—may He be praised and exalted—be free of all such dependence. [156]

And God—great and glorious—is the Enricher as well. But it is inconceivable that the one who is enriched become in his enrichment absolutely rich, since he will at least be in need of the one who made him rich. So he is not in fact rich, though he is able to dispense with everything but God, but only because He supplies him with what he needs; not because his neediness has been cut off at the roots. The truly rich one has need of nothing at all, while the one who is needy yet possesses what he needs is called rich figuratively. This is the highest possible realization which may be attained by one who is not God—may He be praised and exalted.

So far as losing neediness is concerned, it is not to be. If there is no neediness save for God the most high, he will be called 'rich'. If he had not retained the basis of neediness, the saying of the most High would not be correct: *God is the Rich, and you are the poor* (XLVII:38). But for the fact that it is conceivable that one could become free from everything but God, it would not be correct to ascribe to God most high the attribute of enricher.

90. *Al-Māni*ᶜ—the Protector—is the one who counters the causes of destruction and diminishment in religious and tempo-

ral affairs by creating causes intended for protection. We have already treated the meaning of 'the Preserver' [§39], and all preserving necessarily protects and repels, so whoever understands the meaning of 'preserver' understands the meaning of 'protector'. For protecting is related to the causes of destruction, while preserving is related to being freed from destruction, so it is the ultimate goal of protecting. For protecting is desired for preserving, while preserving is not desired for protecting. As a result, every preserver is a protector, but not every protector preserves, except when it is a case of an absolute protector countering all the causes of destruction and diminishment, so that preservation is attained necessarily.

91-92. *Al-Ḍārr, al-Nāfi*ʿ—the Punisher, He who Benefits—is the one from whom comes forth good and evil, benefit and harm, all of which is to be referred to God most high—whether He act by means of angels, men, or inanimate things, [157] or by any other means. Do not suppose that poison kills or harms by itself, or that food satisfies or benefits by itself; or that kings or men or Satan, or any creature—be they heavenly bodies or stars or anything else—are capable of good or evil, benefit or harm, by themselves. For all of these are subservient causes from which nothing proceeds except that for which they were utilized.

All of that is related to the eternal power much as a pen is related to a writer in popular belief. Take the case of the sultan: when he decrees reward or punishment, one does not regard that benefit or harm as coming from the pen but from that to which the pen is subservient; and the other means and causes perform in a similar way. We said 'in popular belief' because ignorant people consider the pen subservient to the writer, but knowledgeable ones understand that it is subservient to the hand of God—may He be praised and exalted—and that He is the one to whom the writer is subservient. For inasmuch as He has created the writer, created the power he has, and establishes definitive motives in him which do not waver in their resolve, the movement of the fingers and of the pen comes forth from him inevitably, whether he wants it or rejects it; in fact it is impossible for him not to will it. So the one who writes, using the man's pen and his hand, is God most high—and if you know this to be the case with an animal possessed of free choice, it is yet more obvious with inanimate things.

93. *Al-Nūr*—Light—is the visible one by whom everything is made visible, for what is visible in itself and makes other things visible is called 'light'. In the measure that existence is opposed to non-existence, what is visible cannot but be linked to existence, for no darkness is darker than non-existence. What is free from the darkness of non-existence, and even from the possibility of non-existence, who draws everything from the darkness of non-existence to the manifestation of existence, is worthy of being named light. Existence is a light streaming to all things from the light of His essence, for He [158] *is the light of the heavens and the earth.* And as there is not an atom of the light of the sun which does not by itself lead one to the existence of the sun which illuminates it, so there is not a single atom from the existents of the heavens and the earth and what lies between them which does not lead one by the very possibility of its existence to the necessary existence who brings them into being. What we have remarked about the meaning of the Manifest [§75] will help you understand the meaning of light, and will allow you to dispense with the arbitrary remarks made about its meaning.

94. *Al-Hādī*—the Guide—is the one who guides the elect among His servants to a knowledge of His essence so they might call upon it as a witness to things, as He guides the bulk of His servants to the things He has created so they might call upon them as a witness to His essence, as well as guiding each created thing to what it needs to satisfy its needs. So He guides the

infant to take the breast from the moment of its release from the womb, He guides the young bird to pick up seeds at the time of its coming out of the shell, and He guides the bee to build his house in a hexagonal shape, as being the shape most suitable to his body, the most cohesive shape and the one least likely to be pierced by damaging holes. To explain that would take too long, but the saying of the Most High expresses it: *Who gave unto everything its nature, then guided it aright* (XX:50), and *Who measures, then guides* (LXXXVII:3).

The ones who guide among men are the prophets and scholars who direct creatures to happiness in the world to come, and guide them to the straight path of God. But it is God who guides them in what they say, and they are subservient to His power and planning.

95. *Al-Badīʿ*—the Absolute cause—is such that nothing similar to it is known. And if nothing is known to be similar to it—not in its essence nor in its attributes or in its action, nor in anything attributed to it, that one is the absolutely original. [159] Were something known to be like that one, it would not be the absolutely original. Nothing befits this name absolutely but God—may He be praised and exalted, for there is no-one before Him so that one like Him could be known before Him. Furthermore, every existing thing that comes after Him is realized by His origination, and is hence incommensurate with its maker—so He is originator eternally and forever.

Every man who is marked by a special characteristic, in prophecy, sainthood, or knowledge, such that none like him is known either in times gone by or in his generation, is original in relation to what is peculiarly his, and in the time to which he belongs.

96. *Al-Bāqī*—the Everlasting—is the existent whose existence is necessary in itself. When the mind relates it to the future, it is called 'everlasting', and when it is related to the past

it is called 'eternal' [*qadīm*]. The everlasting is such that the projection of its existence into the future has no end, but so it is declared to be forever [*abadī*]; while the absolutely eternal is one whose existence into the past does not finally terminate in a first moment, and so it is declared to be eternal [*azalī*]. Now your saying: 'the existence necessary in itself' embraces all that, so these names are employed only to the extent that the mind relates this necessary existence to past or future.

Yet only changeable things participate in past or future, because past or future are temporal expressions; and only change or motion participate in time, since motion is divided into past and future, and changeable things participate in time by means of change [i.e., motion]. So what is above change and motion is not in time, and past or future has no part in it, so [160] in such things passing is no different from enduring. For past and future are only real for us when things have elapsed for us or in us, or when new things will occur. It is necessary that things happen one after another so that they can be divided into a past which has already ceased to exist and is over, a present which is current, and that whose later renewal is expected. So to the extent that there is no renewal or no expiration, there is no time.

How could this be otherwise? For the Truth—may He be praised and exalted—was before time, and to the extent that He created time, is not at all changed in His essence. For before He created time, time did not apply to Him, and after creating time He continued as He had been. So whoever said: 'Duration is a quality additional to the essence of the everlasting' is far afield; and even father afield is the one who said: 'Pre-existence is a quality additional to the essence of the eternal [*qadīm*]'. The best proof you can have of the incorrectness of this view is the folly which results in considering the everlasting character of the everlasting and the everlasting character of the attributes, as well as the pre-existence of the eternal and the pre-existence of the attributes.[95]

97. *Al-Wārith*—the Inheritor—is the one to whom possessions return after the possessors disappear, and that is God—may He be praised and exalted, since He is the one who endures after the creation vanishes, and all things return to Him as their end result. He is the one who asks at that time: '*Who takes possession today?*' and He is the one who answers: '*That belongs to God, one and prevailing*'(XL:16). And this is said in the face of the opinion of most people, for they think they have both property and possession, and on that day the true situation will be revealed to them: this announcement expresses the truth which will be disclosed to them at that time. Now those endowed with spiritual perception have always realized the meaning of this announcement, hearing it without benefit of sound or letters, certain that possession belongs to God—one and prevailing—in every moment of every hour of every [161] day, and that He has been thus always, and shall be so eternally. But this is grasped only by one who perceives the truth of divine unity [*tawḥīd*] in the work [of creation], and knows that the solitary one at work in power and sovereignty is One. But we have explained that in the beginning of the *Kitāb al-Tawakkul* in *Iḥyā' ʿUlūm al-Dīn* [*Revival of the Religious Sciences*]. Let it be sought there, for this book cannot contain it.

98. *Al-Rashīd*—the Right in Guidance—is the one whose plans are ordered to their goals according to approved ways of acting without any indication of an advisor or the directions of a director or the guidance of a guide. And He is God—may He be praised and exalted. Every man is rightly guided in the measure that he is directed by right reason in the plans he makes to assimilate himself to God with regard to his intentions, his religious duties, and his worldly affairs.

99. *Al-Ṣabūr*—the Patient—is the one who does not let haste move him to carry out an action before its time, but rather decides matters according to definite plan, and brings

them about in delineated ways; not keeping them from their appointed time as a lazy person would do by procrastinating, nor bringing them forth before their time as a precipitate person would by hastening—but rather disposing each thing in its proper time, in the way in which it needs to be and according to what it requires. And all that without being subjected to a force opposing His will.

So far as man's patience is concerned, it will require endurance, since the meaning of patience for him involves affirming religious or rational resolve in opposing the impulses of passion or anger. And if two opposing motives contend for him, and he repels the impulse leading to rashness and haste yet inclines to the one inducing him to delay, he will be called patient, since he caused the impulse to haste to be overcome. In the case of God—may He be praised—inclination to haste is non-existent; so far as haste is concerned, He is farther from it than anyone in whom an inclination exists [162] yet is overcome, so He is the one most deserving of this name—after one has removed from consideration any conflict of inclinations or any need to overcome them by way of exertion.

## EPILOGUE TO THIS CHAPTER, AND AN APOLOGY

You should know that it was the saying of the Messenger of God—God's blessing and peace be upon him—which brought me to mention these counsels following the names and attributes: 'You should be characterized by the characteristics of God most high'; as well as his saying—may peace and blessing be upon him: 'Given that God is characterized by the ninety-nine [names], whoever is characterized by one of them enters paradise'.[96] Moreover, some expressions frequently on the lips of Sufis point to what we have mentioned, yet in such a way as to suggest to the immature some sense of inherence [*ḥulūl*] and identification [*ittiḥād*].[97] But that is hardly the view of reasonable people, to say nothing of those who are set apart by the special features of mystical vision. In that regard, I heard Shaykh Abū ʿAlī al-Farmadhī relate concerning his shaykh, Abu'l-Qāsim al-Karakānī—may God sanctify the spirits of them both—that he used to say: 'The ninety-nine names become attributes of the servant following the spiritual path, while he is still on the way and has not yet arrived'. If he intended by what he said something comparable to what we have mentioned, then it is sound and one need not suppose anything but that; yet the expression retains a certain latitude and figurativeness since the names are intended as attributes of God most high, and His attributes do not become attributes of anyone else. So the meaning of his saying is that one has attained what is compatible with these attributes, as when one says: someone attained the knowledge of his professor. The knowledge of the professor is not attained by the student, but he does attain something like his knowledge. [163]

Now if anyone thinks that what is intended by what was said is not what we have noted, and that it is definitely wrong, I would say: whoever says that the meanings of the names of God—may He be praised and exalted—become one's attributes must either mean those very attributes or a likeness of them. And if he means a likeness of them, he must either mean a likeness complete in every respect or a likeness of them to the extent of the name and a partaking in the common meaning of the attributes short of their specific [divine] meanings. So these represent two possibilities. Now if he means the actual attributes, that would have to be either by way firstly of transferring the attributes from the Lord to the man. And if not by transferring them, then it would have to be either by assimilating man's essence to the Lord's essence, to the point where the two would be identical and attributes of one would be those of the other, or by way of inherence. These represent three further possibilities: transfer, identification, or inherence.

Of these five possibilities, only one of them is sound: that which asserts of a man things related to the generic meaning of these attributes, which share the name with them yet are not a perfect likeness of them, as we noted in the counsels accompanying each name.

So far as the second possibility is concerned: that actual likenesses of them be truly affirmed of a man; that would be impossible. For among them would be a knowledge by which he would comprehend all objects so that *he would not miss an atom on earth or in the heavens* (XXXIV:3), and he would have a single power encompassing all objects to the point of being thereby creator of earth and heaven and all that is between them.[98] But how can this be conceived of anyone other than God the most high? And how could man be creator of the heavens [164] and the earth and all that is between them when he is among those things that are between them? How can he be creator of himself? Moreover, if you asserted these attributes of two men, each of them would be creator of the other, so that each one would be creator with respect to the one creating him—and all such statements are farcical and impossible.

So far as the third possibility is concerned, that the actual divine attributes be transferred, that is impossible as well, since it is impossible to separate attributes from what they characterize. Nor is this peculiar to the pre-eternal essence, for it is inconceivable that Zayd's very knowledge be transferred to ʿAmr, since attributes only subsist as properties of subjects. Yet because transferring requires the thing from which the transfer was made to become empty, the essence from which the divine attributes were transferred would necessarily be left naked, and it would be stripped of its divinity. And that is an obvious impossibility as well.

Regarding the fourth possibility, that of identification, that is even more obviously false, since whoever asserts that man becomes identical with the Lord utters a self-contradictory expression. Instead it behooves us to remove the Lord—may

He be praised and exalted—far above impossibilities like these which may be said of Him. So we insist most emphatically that whoever says that one thing becomes another thing is uttering an absolute impossibility. Let us say why: If Zayd is conceived to be one, and ʿAmr is conceived to be one, and then it is said that Zayd becomes ʿAmr and is assimilated to him, then it must be that when they are assimilated one to the other, that both of them will exist or neither of them will, or that Zayd will exist and ʿAmr not, or vice-versa. There is no possibility beyond these four. [165]

Now if they are two existents, the individuality of one of them cannot become the individuality of the other, since the individuality of each of them is an existent. They could at most occupy the same space, yet that would not require identification of one with the other. Indeed, knowledge, will, and power might be joined in one essence, without having different places; nevertheless power is not knowledge or will; nor is one identical with the other.

If neither of them exists, then there is no identification but rather an annihilation; or perhaps the emergence of a third thing.

And if one of them does not exist and the other does, there is no identification, since an existent cannot be united with nothing. So identification between two things is utterly impossible, and this applies to similar essences, to say nothing of different ones. So as it is impossible for this blackness to become that blackness, it is also impossible for this blackness to become that whiteness or this knowledge. And the differences between man and the Lord are even greater than those between blackness and knowledge.

So the principle of identification is false, so that when identification is invoked and one says: 'this is identical with that',[99] it is only by way of the loose and figurative speech appropriate to the usages of Sufis and poets. For they follow the path of figurative speech for the sake of enhancing the way the word strikes the understanding—as when the poet says: 'I am whom I desire and the one I desire is I'. That is to be explained from the poet's perspective, but he does not mean that he is actually the other, but that it is as though he were he. He is immersed in concern for him as he might be immersed in concern for himself, so he expresses this condition of assimilation by way of a figure of speech. [166]

The saying of Abū Yazīd—may God be merciful to him—ought to be taken in a similar way: 'I have sloughed off myself as the snake sloughs off its skin, and I looked and behold! I am He'.[100] Now his meaning is that when one sloughs off the passions of his soul with its desires and concerns, no room remains in him for anything other than God, nor will he have any concern other than God—may He be praised and exalted. So if nothing exists in his heart but the majesty of God and His beauty, so that he becomes immersed in it, he does become as though he were He, but not so that he actually is God. And there is a difference between our saying 'as though he were He' and our saying 'he is He'. But we may use our saying 'he is he' to express our saying 'he is as though he were he', just as the poet sometimes says 'as though I were the one I desire' and sometimes 'I am the one I desire'. But here lies a pitfall, for if one does not have a firm footing in things rational, he may fail to distinguish one of them from the other, and looking upon the perfection of his essence and how it may be adorned with the finery of truth which shines in it, he will think that he is He [God], and will say: 'I am the Truth'.[101]

Such a one commits the same error as the Christians, when they see that [same perfection] in the essence of the messiah, ʿĪsā [Jesus]—may peace be upon him—and say: he is God; yet they are as mistaken as the one who looks into a mirror and sees in it a coloured image yet thinks that this image is the image of the mirror, and this colour is the colour of the mirror. Far from it! For the mirror has no colour in itself; its nature is rather to receive the image of coloured things in such a way as to display them to those looking at the appearance of things as though they were the images of the mirror—to the point where a child who sees a man in the mirror thinks that the man [167] actually is in the mirror. In a similar way, the heart is devoid of images and shapes in itself, yet its state is to receive the meaning of shapes and images and realities. So whatever inheres in it is as though it were identical with it, but it is not actually identical with it. Similarly, one unfamiliar with glass or wine, when he sees the glass with wine in it may not notice the difference between them, and sometimes he will say: 'there is no wine', and sometimes 'there is no glass'. The poet expressed this when he said:

> The glass is fine and the wine is pure,
> So alike are they that the facts are confused;
>
> As if there were wine and no glass,
> Or a glass and no wine.[102]

Now the claim of the one who said 'I am the Truth' either means what the poet means when he said: 'I am whom I desire, and the one I desire is I', or he says it in error, as Christians err in thinking that divinity is united with humanity in Jesus. So with the saying of Abū Yazīd—may God be merciful to him—(if in fact it be his): 'May I be praised, for how exalted is my nature!' It could be (1) that it proceeded from his tongue in circumstances of reporting the speech of God—great and glorious—as though he had been overheard reciting: '*There is no God save Me, so serve Me*' (xx:14), and so could be interpreted as reported speech.[103] Or (2) he could have noticed the perfection of his share in the attribute of holiness, as we remarked concerning one's rising by knowledge above things imagined or sensed, or above pleasures and passions by determination; so he spoke of the holiness of his soul when he said: 'May I be praised!' And he may have seen the greatness of his nature by comparison with the nature of common people when he said: 'How exalted is my nature!'

Yet in spite of that he knew that he was holy and his nature exalted only by comparison with the rest of people, and not in relation to the holiness of the Lord—the most high [168] and holy One—or the immensity of His nature. Furthermore, it might have been the case that he emitted this utterance in his inebriation and in the ecstasies of his state, and that returning to sobriety and a balanced state demanded caution regarding suggestive utterances, something the state of inebriation may not be able to muster. But if you were to disregard these two interpretations in favour of identification, then that would make the statement utterly impossible. And one ought not regard the positions of men so highly so as to give credence to what is impossible; it rather behooves us to know men by the truth than the truth by men. Regarding the fifth possibility, that of inherence [*ḥulūl*], that is, the conception of one who says that the Lord—may He be blessed and exalted—inheres in man, or that man inheres in the Lord: may the Lord of Lords be exalted well beyond the sayings of evildoers! This saying, even if it were true, would not demand identification nor require that men be characterized by the attributes of the Lord, for the attributes of the one inhering do not become the attributes of the one in whom he inheres. Rather, the attributes of the one who inheres remain as they were. The sense in which inherence is impossible will only be understood after one understands the meaning of inherence, for with such specialized notions, if one does not grasp them by means of some illustration, it is hardly possible to know how to affirm or deny them. If one does not understand the meaning of *inherence*, how can one know whether inherence is a fact or an impossibility?

We say that 'inherence' signifies two things. One of them is the relation which holds between bodies and the space they occupy, yet that only obtains between two bodies. Whatever is free from any notion of bodiliness cannot conform to that case. Secondly, it signifies the relation holding between [169] accident and substance. Now accidents have their subsistence in substance, and this may be expressed by saying that they inhere in it, and that is impossible for anything which subsists in itself. So far be it from us to mention the Lord—the most high and holy One—in this context, since it is impossible that anything which subsists in itself inhere in something subsisting in itself—except by way of the proximity among bodies. So inherence between men is inconceivable; how then can it be conceived between man and the Lord?

So if inherence, transference, identification, and being characterized by [exact] likenesses of the attributes of God—may He be praised and exalted—are all, in truth, invalid, the only meaning which remains from all they have offered is the one we have indicated in the 'counsels' accompanying each name. And that blocks the absolute saying that the meanings of the names of God most high become attributes of men—except as qualified by reservations free from ambiguity; otherwise the absolute use of this utterance is misleading.

You may ask: what does it mean to say that man is still on the way and has not yet arrived, even though he be characterized by all that? What does 'on the way' or 'arrived' mean here?[104] You should know that 'being on the way' involves refining one's character, actions, and knowledge, and that means being occupied with one's formation, externally and interiorly. In all this a man is occupied with himself rather than his Lord—may He be praised and exalted—even though he be taken up with the formation of his inner self, in preparation for 'arriving'. The one who arrives is one to whom the clarity of truth is revealed, and who has become immersed in it. If his knowledge be considered, he knows none but God; and if his determination be considered, he has ambition for none but God. So all of him is taken up with the whole of Him, in witnessing and in concern, and so not occupied with himself—either externally in actions of worship or interiorly in refining his character.[105] All of that is geared to purity, and it is the beginning, while the end

[170] lies in being stripped of oneself totally, and to be devoted to Him—so that it is as though he were He, and that is 'arriving' [or 'attainment'].[106]

Now you might say: the words of the Sufis are based on visions revealed to them in the 'stage of friendship' [*ṭawr al-wilāya*], and reason falls short of grasping that, yet all that you have said involves the exercise of the powers of reason.[107] Yet you should know that it is not possible for one to see in the stage of friendship anything which reason judges to be impossible. Certainly, it is possible for one to see something which exceeds reason, in the sense that one will not grasp it by reason alone. For example, it may be revealed to a holy man that someone will die tomorrow, and that would not be known by the powers of reason because reason falls short of it. But it is not possible that it be revealed that God—may He be praised and exalted—will create tomorrow someone like Himself, for reason shows that to be contrary to it, rather than exceeding it. And even farther from the mark than that would be to say that God—may He be blessed and exalted—will make me like Himself. And yet more far-fetched than this would be to say that God—great and glorious—would make me become Himself, that is, that I would become He; for this could only mean that I am a creature yet God—the most high and holy One—makes me eternal, and while I am not creator of the heavens and earth, God makes me creator of heaven and earth. This is the meaning of his saying: 'I looked and behold! I am He', if it is not interpreted. Whoever believes things like this has forfeited the power of reason, and can no longer distinguish what he knows from what he does not know, so he might as well believe that it could be revealed to a holy man that the *sharīʿa* [the divine law] is false, or that, even if it were true, that God could change it [171] and make it false, or that He could make all of the sayings of the prophets false. Now if someone says: the impossibility of changing truth into a lie is only asserted by the power of reason, we must answer that changing truth into falsehood is no more remote than changing a creature into something eternal, or man into the Lord. Whoever cannot distinguish what contradicts reason from what reason cannot attain is beneath being addressed, so let him be left in his ignorance.[108]

## CHAPTER TWO [172]

# Concerning the Meanings [of the Names], Offering an Explanation how these many names resolve to the Essence with seven Attributes, according to the people of the *Sunna*

PERHAPS you will say: there are many names here, and you have kept them from being synonymous and demanded that each one comprise a distinct meaning, so how will you resolve all of them to seven attributes?[109] You should know that if there be seven attributes, there are still many actions and many attributes, the totality of which almost exceeds enumeration. Moreover, it is possible to make a composite from the sum of two attributes, or from an attribute with something added, or from an attribute with a negation, or from (4) an attribute with a negation and something added; and then posit a name corresponding to each one so as to increase the number of names. And the totality of them may be resolved into those which indicate (1) the essence, (2) the essence with a negation, (3) the essence with something added, (5) one of the seven attributes, an attribute with negation, (6,7,8) an attribute with something added, (9) an attribute of action (10) with something added or negated—and these make ten possibilities.[110]

First: what indicates the essence, as in your saying 'Allāh'. And the name 'the Truth' [*al-Ḥaqq*] is close to it, since that means the essence in so far as it is necessary existence.[111]

Second: what indicates the essence with a negation, like 'the Holy' [*al-Quddūs*], 'the Flawless' [*al-Salām*], 'the Rich' [*al-Ghanī*], 'the One' [cf. §76; *al-Wāḥid*], and those like them. For 'the Holy' is one from whom everything which occurs to one's mind [173] or enters into the imagination has been negated, as 'the Flawless' is one from whom all defects have been negated, and 'the Rich' is one devoid of need, while 'the One' is deprived of a similar or of divisibility.

Third: what refers to the essence with something added, like 'the Most High' [*al-ʿAlī*], 'the Tremendous' [*al-ʿAẓīm*], 'the First' [*al-Awwal*], 'the Last' [*al-Ākhir*], 'the Manifest' [*al-Ẓāhir*], 'the Hidden' [*al-Bāṭin*], and those like them. So 'the Most High' is the essence whose degree is above the general run of essences, therefore it is in addition to them; and 'the Tremendous' refers to the essence insofar as the limits of perception are transcended; while 'the First' comes before all existing things, and 'the Last' is the one who is subsequent to the final end of existing things. 'The Manifest' is the essence with respect to demonstrations of reason, and 'the Hidden' is the essence as it relates to perceptions of sense and imagination. Look for the rest in this way.

Fourth: what refers to the essence with negation and addition, like 'the King' [*al-Malik*] or 'the Eminent' [*al-ʿAzīz*]. 'The King' refers to an essence which needs nothing while everything needs it, and 'the Eminent' is one whom nothing is like and one whose level is difficult to attain or to achieve.

Fifth: what refers to an attribute, like 'the Omniscient' [*al-ʿAlīm*], 'the All-Powerful' [*al-Qādir*], 'the Living' [*al-Ḥayy*], 'the All-Hearing' [*al-Samīʿ*], 'the All-Seeing' [*al-Baṣīr*].

Sixth: what refers to knowing with something in addition, like 'the Wise' [*al-Ḥakīm*], 'The Totally Aware' [*al-Khabīr*], 'the Universal Witness' [*al-Shahīd*], and 'the Knower of each separate thing' [*al-Muḥṣī*]. For 'The Totally Aware' refers to knowledge in relation to hidden things, and 'the Universal Witness' refers to knowledge in relation to what can be seen, and 'the Wise' refers to knowledge in relation to the most noble objects, while 'the Knower of each separate thing' refers to knowledge insofar as it comprehends objects limited to what is countable in detail.

Seventh: what refers to power with something more added, like 'the Dominator' [*al-Qahhār*], 'the Strong' [*al-Qawī*], 'the all-Determiner' [*al-Muqtadir*], [174] and 'the Firm' [*al-Matīn*]. Now strength is the perfection of power, and firmness its intensification, while dominating is its effect in being able to conquer.

Eighth: what refers to will with something added or in connection with action, like 'the Infinitely Good' [*al-Raḥmān*], 'the Merciful' [*al-Raḥīm*], 'the All-Pitying' [*al-Ra'ūf*], and 'the Loving-kind' [*al-Wadūd*]. These refer to will in relation to good deeds or fulfilling the needs of the weak, and you have come to know what that involves.

Ninth: what refers to attributes of action, like 'the Creator' [*al-Khāliq*], 'the Producer' [*al-Bāri'*], 'the Fashioner' [*al-Muṣawwir*], 'the Bestower' [*al-Wahhāb*], 'the Provider' [*al-Razzāq*], 'the Opener' [*al-Fattāḥ*], 'He who contracts' [*al-Qābiḍ*], 'He who expands' [*al-Bāsiṭ*], 'the Abaser' [*al-Khāfiḍ*], 'the Exalter' [*al-Rāfiᶜ*], 'the Honourer' [*al-Muᶜizz*], 'He who humbles' [*al-Mudhill*], 'the Just' [*al-ᶜAdl*], 'the Nourisher' [*al-Muqīt*], 'the Life Giver' [*al-Muḥyī*], 'the Slayer' [*al-Mumīt*], 'the Promoter' [*al-Muqaddim*], 'the Postponer' [*al-Mu'akhkhir*], 'the Ruler' [*al-Wālī*], 'the Doer of Good' [*al-Barr*], 'the Ever-Relenting' [*al-Tawwāb*], 'the Avenger' [*al-Muntaqim*], 'the Equitable' [*al-Muqsiṭ*], 'the Uniter' [*al-Jāmiᶜ*], 'the Protector' [*al-Māniᶜ*], 'the Enricher' [*al-Mughnī*], 'the Guide' [*al-Hādī*], and those like them.

Tenth: what refers to an indication of action with something more, like 'the All-Glorious' [*al-Majīd*], 'the Generous' [*al-Karīm*], and 'the Benevolent' [*al-Laṭīf*]. For 'the All-Glorious' refers to an abundance of kindness together with nobility of essence, and likewise for 'the Generous', while 'the Benevolent' refers to gentleness in action.

These names and the rest of them do not go beyond the sum of these ten possibilities. Compare what we have not mentioned with what we have, for that indicates the way in which the names are free from synonymy while resolving them to these few well-known attributes. [175]

## CHAPTER THREE

# Offering an explanation how all of these attributes resolve to a single essence, according to the teaching of the Muʿtazilites and the philosophers

WHILE this chapter is not really appropriate to this book, we nonetheless offer this brief treatment in response to a request. Should anyone wish that it not be included in this book, he may drop it, since it is of no importance to [the argument] of the book.

Now I say: although those people [Muʿtazilites and philosophers] deny the attributes and only assert a single essence in God, they do not deny His actions nor a multiplicity of negations or additions [to it]. Moreover, they are sympathetic to what we have repeated concerning the names according to these ten possibilities.

Regarding the seven attributes, which are life, knowledge, power, will, hearing, seeing, and speaking, they contend that all of these resolve to knowledge, and then that knowledge resolves to the essence. The explanation they offer is that hearing is the same as His perfect knowledge with regard to sound, and sight is the same as His knowledge with regard to colour and other things seen. Furthermore, according to them, speech resolves to His action, and according to the Muʿtazilites comprises the words which He creates in matter from inanimate materials, while the philosophers resolve it to the hearing which He creates in the essence of the Prophet—may God's blessing and peace be upon him, so that he hears ordered speech as a sleeping person might hear it, without its coming to him from outside.[112] And that is attributed to God most high, in the sense that it is not realized in the Prophet by the action of human beings and the sounds they make. Regarding life, they contend that it is the same as God's knowledge by His essence [176] because whatever knows by its essence is said to be alive, while whatever does not know by its essence is not called 'living'.

So only 'will' and 'power' remain. They contend that the meaning of 'will' consists in His—the most high and holy one's—knowing the *ratio* of the good and its order so that good exists as He knows it. So His knowledge of a thing is the cause of that thing's existence: when He knows the good proper to a thing it will be achieved, and if there be nothing repugnant in it, He will be satisfied. And whoever is satisfied may be said to have willed, and hence will can be resolved to knowledge without repugnance. So far as power is concerned, it means that He acts or not, as He wills. Now His action is something known, and His willing resolves to His knowledge of the *ratio* of the good. So 'willing' simply means that whatever He knows would be good to exist will be created by Him, and whatever He knows will not be good to exist will not be created.[113] The order of the good [*bonum ordinis*] needs only His knowledge of it to exist, just as whatever does not exist owes the fact that it does not exist to the absence of His knowing that there is good in its existing. Rational order is the cause of the actual order, and the actual order complies with rational order.

They claim that our knowledge only needs power to realize what it knows, because our action only takes place through the body, so it is necessary that the body be sound and characterized by strength. But He does not make use of a body, so His knowledge suffices to bring what He knows into existence. So power also resolves to knowledge.

Then they claim that knowledge in turn resolves to His essence. For He knows His essence by His essence; and knowledge, knower, and thing known are one.[114] He only knows what is other than Himself by His essence, since He knows His essence to be the source of every existing thing, and He knows that all existing things come from His essence by way of dependence, [177] yet this does not imply multiplicity in His essence.[115]

They contend that the knowledge the One has (which is His essence) is related to the multiplicity of objects known, much like the knowledge of an accountant when he is asked: what is the double of two, and the double of the double, and the double of that double?—and so on like that for ten times. Before setting these doubles out in detail in his mind, he is certain of what he will arrive at, given what he already knows. That certainty is the source of the detailed exposition when he undertakes it, for that very certainty is a single guiding principle related to all the doublings of two, even to an infinity of such doubles, without any need to elaborate it in detail. And just as the doubling of two proceeds towards multiplicity by degrees, so it is with existing things among which an order can be found: there is no multiplicity in the first of them, but they call each other forth to multiplicity by degrees.

To explain that and to refute it would take too long, so let me appeal to what we have said about it in *Kitāb al-Tahāfut*, for it remains far from the intent of this book—and God knows best.[116]

## PART THREE

CHAPTER ONE [181]

# On explaining that the names of God most high are not limited to ninety-nine so far as divine instruction is concerned

INDEED, divine instruction mentions names other than the ninety-nine, since in another version given on the authority of Abū Hurayra—may the Lord be pleased with him—names close to these names were substituted for some of them and even some which are not so close. Regarding the ones close in meaning, *al-Aḥad* (the One) was substituted for *al-Wāḥid* (the Unique), *al-Qāhir* (the Conqueror) for *al-Qahhār* (the Dominator), *al-Shākir* (the Thankful) for *al-Shakūr* (the Grateful). Ones not so close in meaning were also substituted, like *al-Hādī* (the Guide), *al-Kāfī* (the One who suffices), *al-Dā'im* (the Enduring), *al-Baṣīr* (the Insightful), *al-Nūr al-Mubīn* (the Clear Light), *al-Jamīl* (the Beautiful), *al-Ṣādiq* (the Truthful), *al-Muḥīt* (the Comprehending), *al-Qarīb* (the Close), *al-Qadīm* (the Everlasting), *al-Witr* (the Un-even), *al-Fāṭir* (the Creator), *al-ʿAllām* (the All-Knowing), *al-Mulk* (the Sovereignty),[1] *al-Akram* (the most Generous), *al-Mudabbir* (the Director), *al-Rafīʿ* (the Elevated), *Dhū'l-ṭawl* (the Lord of Height), *Dhū'l-Maʿārij* (the Lord of the Ascenders), *Dhū'l-Faḍl* (the Lord of Benefit), and *al-Khallāq* (the Maker).

Furthermore, names are noted in the Qur'ān which do not match with either of the two lists, like *al-Mawlā* (the Master), *al-*

*Naṣīr* (the Protector), *al-Ghālib* (the Victor), *al-Qarīb* (the Close), *al-Rabb* (the Lord), and *al-Nāṣir* (the Deliverer). And there are compound expressions as well, such as in the Most High's saying: *witness of retribution, receiver of repentance, forgiver of sins, merger of night into day, merger of day into night, bringer of life from death,* and *bringer of death from life.*

Moreover, *al-Sayyid* (the Master) is also mentioned in a report: when a man once addressed the messenger of God—may God's blessing and peace be upon him: 'O master', and he said: 'The Master is God—great and glorious'.[2] This was as though he meant to forbid any praise in his presence, yet otherwise he had said—may God's blessing and peace be upon him: 'I am master of the sons of Adam and I say this without boasting'.[3] *Al-Dayyān* is also mentioned, as well as *al-Ḥannān, al-Mannān,* and others like them, which could be found were one to look them up in the *ḥadīth.* [182]

Furthermore, actions associated with God most high in the Qur'ān are numerous, for it is said of Him: *He removes the evil* (XXVII:62), *He hurls the truth* (XXXIV:48), *He will distinguish between them* (XXXII:25), and *We decreed for the children of Israel* (XVII:4). So if deriving names from actions be permitted, then one may derive as His names: 'the Remover', 'the Hurler of Truth', 'the Distinguisher', and 'the One who Decrees'. Yet such names from the Qur'ān are countless, as will be shown later.

Our purpose is to show that the names are not identical with the ninety-nine which we have enumerated and explained, but we have followed customary usage in explaining these names, for it is they which appear in the well-known version. Moreover, these modifications and elaborations transmitted on the authority of Abū Hurayra are not found in the two most attested books of *ḥadīth* [*al-ṣaḥīḥayn*]; rather, the attested books only contain the names of which he says—may God's blessing and peace be upon him: 'God—may He be praised and exalted—has ninety-nine names, and whoever enumerates them enters paradise'.[4] But they were not specified and elaborated in these genuine *ḥadīths*.

Some names upon which jurisprudents and scholars have agreed are: 'the Willer', 'the Speaker', 'the Existent', 'the Thing', 'the Everlasting Essence', and 'the Eternal'. These are things which one is permitted to use of God—may He be praised and exalted. Now it is noted in the *ḥadīth*: 'Do not say "Ramaḍān is coming", for "Ramaḍān" is a name of God most high. Say rather "the month of Ramaḍān is coming".'[5] Similarly, it is reported that the messenger of God—may God's blessing and peace be upon him—said: 'Whatever distress or affliction that befalls a person, let him say: "O God, I am Your servant, and the son of Your servant, and the son of Your bondsmaid: my forelock [183] is in Your hand, Your judgment concerning me is done. I implore You by every name which is Yours, by which You have named Yourself, or which You revealed in Your book, or which You taught to anyone from Your creation, or which You appropriated to Yourself in Your knowledge of hidden things, that You might make the Qur'ān a renewal of my heart, a light for my inmost thoughts, a way through my affliction, and the unravelling of my distress"; and God—great and glorious—will remove his distress and affliction, and replace them with happiness'.[6] And his saying 'which You appropriated to Yourself in Your knowledge of hidden things' shows that the names are not limited to those mentioned in the well-known versions. Yet in this regard it may occur to you to question the advantage of limiting the names to ninety-nine. So it behooves us to discuss that. [184]

CHAPTER TWO

# Explaining the advantage of enumerating the names and of specifying them as ninety-nine. In this chapter we will also offer reflections on some things in the form of questions

SOMEONE may well ask about the names of God—may He be praised and exalted: do they exceed ninety-nine or not? And if they do, what is the significance of this specification? When someone possesses a thousand dirhams a reasonable man would not say that he has ninety-nine dirhams just because a thousand includes ninety-nine, for although the thousand does indeed include this, when a specific number is mentioned, this causes one to have the understanding that no number follows it. Yet if the names did not exceed this number, what would his saying mean—may God's blessing and peace be upon him: 'I implore You by every name which is Yours, by which You have named Yourself, or which You revealed in Your book, or which You taught to anyone from Your creation, or which You appropriated to Yourself in Your knowledge of hidden things'?[7] For this makes it clear that God appropriated certain names [and has not informed us of these], as in the case where he said that 'Ramaḍān' is one of the names of God. For this reason, our forefathers used to say: someone was given the greatest name [*al-ism al-aʿẓam*], and that was attributed to some prophets and holy men.[8] This indicates that the greatest name lies outside the ninety-nine. [185]

So we say: thanks to these accounts, it appears more likely that the names exceed ninety-nine. And so far as the *ḥadīth* which mentions the restriction is concerned, it affects one of the points but not both of them [see next paragraph]. It is like the king who has a thousand servants: one could say that the king has ninety-nine servants, and were one to seek their assistance, no enemy could oppose him. What is specified is the number required to obtain the assistance one needs from them, either because of the addition of their strength, or because that number would suffice to repel the enemy without needing any more; it does not specify that only they exist.

It is conceivable that the names not exceed this number. For the statement given in the account includes two points: first, that God the most high has ninety-nine names; and second, that whoever enumerates them enters paradise. Were one to limit oneself to mentioning the first point, the matter would be finished, yet according to the predominant view, it is not possible to limit oneself to mentioning the first point.

This is what comes to mind initially on the basis of the appearance of this restriction, yet it is unlikely for two reasons. First, this interpretation would keep what God appropriates to His knowing of hidden things from counting as one of His names, and the *ḥadīth* asserts as much. Secondly, this interpretation leads to making enumeration of the names the prerogative of a prophet or holy man, who would be given the greatest name by which the number would be completed. For it is either the case that whatever is enumerated without that name falls short of the requisite number, or that the greatest name lies outside that number, so that the enumeration is invalidated by it. But it is more probable that the prophet of God—may God's blessing and peace be upon him—uttered this saying by way of awakening a desire in the people to enumerate the names, yet the people had no knowledge of the greatest name. [186]

Now it may be said: if it is more probable that the names exceed ninety-nine, and we were to estimate, for example, that there were a thousand names, yet whoever enumerated ninety-nine of them would be deserving of paradise, would these be a specific ninety-nine; or would any ninety-nine of them be such that whoever managed to enumerate them would deserve to enter paradise? In either case it would turn out that whoever enumerates once what Abū Hurayra has listed will enter paradise, or if one were to enumerate the ones which the second version contained he also would enter paradise, if we determine that everything in both versions comprises a name of God. So we say: it is more probable that it is a specific ninety-nine which are intended, since if they were not specified, the benefit of the enumeration and the specification would hardly be clear. The statement that the king has a hundred servants such that if one were to seek their assistance no enemy could oppose him, only makes sense if among the many servants the king has, there are a hundred of them distinguished by superior strength and passion for combat. If, however, one might accomplish this with any one hundred servants, the phrasing of the statement would not be appropriate.

Now it may be asked: why is it that ninety-nine of the names have been singled out for a peculiar role in this matter, although all the others are names of God—may He be praised and exalted? We would say: it is possible for names to differ in excellence because their meanings differ in eminence and distinction, so that ninety-nine of them will bring together varieties of meanings which tell of [the divine] majesty which another set of meanings would not be able to bring together, and so that combination is possessed of the greater distinction. [187]

It may be asked: is the greatest name of God included among them or not? If it is not included, how can it be distinguished by greater dignity and yet be outside of the names? Yet if it is included among them, how can that be, for they are a matter of common knowledge while the greatest name is set apart by virtue of its being known by prophets and holy men? Indeed it is said that *Āṣaf* brought the throne of Bilqīs[9] because he had been given the greatest name—itself a source of esteem and greatness for the one who knows it. Our response is that it is possible to say that the greatest name of God is outside this enumeration which Abū Hurayra listed—may God be pleased with him, and that these enumerated names are pre-eminent in relation to the set of names known to the people; not in relation to the names which holy men and prophets know. Yet it is also possible to say that they include the greatest name of God; yet it is hidden among them, and that one does not recognize it on initial examination, since it is told in a *ḥadīth* that the Prophet—may God's blessing and peace be upon him—said: 'the supreme name of God is in these two verses: *Your God is One God; there is no God save Him, the Infinitely Good, the Merciful* (II:163), and the beginning of the sura *Family of ʿImrān: 'Alif. Lām. Mīm. Allāh! there is no God save Him, the Living, the Eternal* (III:1-2)'.[10] It is told that the Prophet of God—may God's blessing and peace be upon him—heard a man praying and saying: 'By God, I ask You that I may bear witness concerning You that You are God and there is no God but You—the eternal One who is neither begotten nor begets and has no one equal to Him'. So he said: 'By the One in whose hand is my soul, he has invoked God most high by His supreme name—the name by which He answers when He is called upon with it, and gives when He is petitioned with it'.[11]

One may ask: what reason can be given for specifying this number as against other ones, and why does it not reach one hundred when it comes so close to it? Our response will indicate two possibilities. First, [188] it may be said that the eminent meanings do not comprise this number because the number was intended, but only because they happened to reach this total. It is like the seven attributes put forward by the *Sunna*: life, knowledge, power, will, hearing, seeing, and speech; they are not specified because they are seven in number, but because it is only by virtue of them that divinity is attained. Secondly, and this is the more evidently correct, the reason for the number is to specify what was mentioned by the prophet of God—may God's blessing and peace be upon him—when he said: 'One hundred minus one, and God who is odd [i.e., one] loves what is odd'.[12] What this indicates, however, is that these names being ninety-nine is a matter of free choice; though not inasmuch as the attributes of eminence are restricted to them, for that pertains to God's essence and is not a matter of willing. So no-one would say that the attributes of God—may He be praised and exalted—are seven because 'He is odd and loves what is odd'; that pertains rather to His essence and His divinity, and there is no restriction on their number. For the divine essence does not exist by virtue of anyone's intending or willing it, as one may intend what is odd to the exclusion of something else; and this comes close to corroborating the possibility which we have mentioned, namely that the names by which God—may He be praised and exalted—names Himself are none other than ninety-nine, and that He does not make them one hundred only because He loves what is odd. We shall show what confirms this possibility.

It may be asked: did the Prophet of God—may God's blessing and peace be upon him—enumerate these ninety-nine names, and intentionally enumerate them to compile them together, or did he leave compiling them to whomever gleaned them from the book [i.e., the Qur'ān] and the *Sunna* and the accounts which contain an indication of them? We would say: the most evidently correct opinion, which is also the best-known, is [189] that this list comprises what the messenger of God enumerated—may God's blessing and peace be upon him, and He compiled them intentionally to bring them together and teach them, according to the narration of Abū Hurayra—may God be pleased with him—since the clear intention of the account is to awaken a desire for enumeration. And that enumeration would have been difficult for the people to do had the messenger of God not explicitly gathered them together. Moreover, this testifies to the soundness of the narration of Abū Hurayra—may God be pleased with him. The people have accepted his well-known version, according to which we have conducted our commentary.

Aḥmad al-Bayhaqī has spoken against the narration of Abū Hurayra, mentioning that weak people are present among its transmitters. And Abū ʿĪsā al-Tirmidhī noted something of the sort in his *Musnad*.[13] Beyond what the compilers of *ḥadīth* have mentioned about it, three things indicate the weakness of this narration. First, there is some confusion [*iḍṭirāb*] in the narration from Abū Hurayra, since we have two narrations from him, and there are manifest differences between them involving substitutions and alterations. Secondly, his narration fails to include mention of 'the Loving' [*al-Ḥannān*], 'the Benefactor' [*al-Mannān*], *Ramaḍān*, and a host of names which appear in the *ḥadīths*. Third, one should note that this number is mentioned in the genuine *ḥadīth*, in his saying—may God's blessing and peace be upon him: that 'God has ninety-nine names and whoever enumerates them enters paradise'. [190] So far as mention of the specific names is concerned, it has not been written in the genuine *ḥadīth* but in an account resting on the authority of one companion which contains weakness in its claim of authority [*isnād*].[14] All of this apparently indicates that the names do not exceed this number. But the absence of some of these names from the version of Abū Hurayra made us incline away from that interpretation. If we had considered weak the version which gives the number of names, a whole quantity of the difficulties would have been removed.

So we say: there are but ninety-nine names by which God—may He be praised and exalted—has named Himself, and they do not reach one hundred because 'He is odd and loves what is odd'. Furthermore, 'the Loving' and 'the Benefactor' and those like them are included in their total. But a knowledge of the totality of them is not possible short of an inquiry into the book [Qur'ān] and the tradition [*Sunna*], since many of them are confirmed in the book of God—may He be praised and exalted—and many of them are in the accounts of *ḥadīth* as well. Nor do I know a single scholar anxious to study them and collect them all, unless it be a certain man from the West who knows a large number of *ḥadīths* by heart, who is called ʿAlī ibn Ḥazm said: 'I have confirmed nearly eighty names contained in the book and genuine accounts, and the remainder need to be sought in the accounts [of *ḥadīth*] by means of independent judgment [*ijtihād*].'[15] I believe that the *ḥadīth* which specifies the number of names did not reach him, or if it did, it seems he considered its authoritative support [*isnād*] to be weak, since he turned away from it towards the accounts mentioned in the authentic collections of *ḥadīth* and to deriving this from them. Based on this, whoever enumerates them—that is, collects and preserves them—will be burdened [191] with hard work in his efforts, and so should be worthy of entering paradise. Otherwise it is easy to enumerate in speech the names which the narration finally recounts. Indeed, the genuine *ḥadīth* record in some phrasings: 'whoever commits them to memory [*ḥifẓ*] enters into paradise',[16] and memorizing them requires increased effort!

These are the possibilities apparent to me concerning this *ḥadīth*. We did not go into most aspects of this, for these are matters of independent judgment which cannot be known without conjecture, and so they are quite far removed from a purely reasonable assessment. Yet God knows best.

## CHAPTER THREE [192]

# Are the names and attributes applied to God—great and glorious—based on divine instruction[17] or permitted on the basis of reason?

What Qāḍī Abū-Bakr[18] preferred was to permit the use of reason except where revelation forbade it or where the sense of an expression would convey something impossible with regard to God—may He be praised and exalted. As for that which contains no forbidding element, it is permissible. Al-Ashʿarī,[19] however, held that it was based on divine instruction, so that it is not permissible to apply to God most high whatever rests on meanings attributed to him, except when it is authorized. As for us, the position which we think better is to distinguish and to say: whatever pertains to names is based on authorization, whereas whatever pertains to attributes is not based on authorization; rather, the ones that are authentic are acceptable, but not the false ones. But this will not be understood until the difference between a name and an attribute is understood.

We say that a name is an utterance imposed to indicate the thing named.[20] Take Zayd, for example: his name is Zayd yet he is in fact fair and tall. So if someone were to say to him: 'O tall one! O fair one!' they would be addressing him by what is attributed to him and would be correct; but that would forego using his name, for his name is Zayd and not the-tall-one nor the-fair-one.[21] For being tall or fair does not mean that 'tall' is his name. Indeed, our naming a boy Qāsim or Jāmiʿ does not mean that he can be described by the meanings of these names.[22] Rather, these names—even when they happen to convey a meaning—simply refer, as do Zayd, ʿĪsā and others which convey no meaning at all.[23] Even if we name him ʿAbd al-Malik, we do not [193] mean that he is the servant of the king. And for that reason we treat ʿAbd al-Malik as a single term, like ʿĪsā and Zayd, whereas if it were used as a description it would be a compound term. Similarly with ʿAbdullāh (servant-of-God), where we form its plural by a single word *ʿAbādila* rather than two: *ʿIbād Allāh*.[24]

When you grasp what a name is, you will see that each individual's name is what he names himself or what anyone with authority over him, such as his father or his master, has named him. So naming, that is, imposing a name, implies a free disposition regarding the one named, and that requires dominion. A man has dominion over himself, his servant, or his child; thus naming is limited to these. Should one impose a name on anyone else, the one named will deny the name and be angered by it. So if it is not up to us to name a human being, that is, to impose a name on him, how can we give names to God most high? Similarly, the names of the Prophet—may God's blessing and peace be upon him—are numbered; he enumerated them when he said: 'I have names: Aḥmad, Muḥammad, al-Muttaqī, al-Māḥī, al-ʿĀqib, Nabī al-Tawbah, Nabī al-Raḥmah, Nabī al-Malḥama'.[25] It is not up to us to add to these so far as naming him is concerned; but so far as recounting his attributes is concerned, it is permissible for us to say that he is a learned man, a counsellor, a discerning man, a true guide, and so on, just as we say of Zayd that he is fair and tall—not as a way of naming him, but as a way of recounting his attributes. In sum, this is a question of jurisprudence since it is an investigation of whether an expression is sanctioned or prohibited.

We say: the evidence that it is forbidden to assign names to God—may He be praised and exalted—[194] is that it is forbidden to assign them to the Prophet—may God's blessing and peace be upon him, except for those he gave to himself or those given him by his Lord or his father. And if it be forbidden with respect to the Prophet—may God's blessing and peace be upon him—or even with respect to any individual creature, it must above all be forbidden with respect to God. This is the sort of juridical analogy on the likes of which judgments regarding divine law are based.[26]

Evidence that attributes are allowed is that they are predicates of something. Predicates are divided into true and false. Revelation has already indicated that whatever is false is proscribed in principle, so whatever is false is forbidden, except in unusual circumstances.[27] It also indicated that true predicates are allowed, so whatever is true is permissible, except in unusual circumstances. If we be permitted to say of Zayd that he exists, so too with God most high, whether revelation mentions it or not. We say that He is eternal, even were we to suppose that revelation did not mention it. Just as we do not say of Zayd that he is tall and light-skinned, because that might reach Zayd and he would take umbrage at it as suggesting a defect, so we do not say anything of God that could suggest any imperfection at all. Now whatever does not suggest imperfection or conveys praise is applicable and permissible, according to the reasoning that permits whatever is true to the extent that there are no circumstances forbidding it.

So it is that one expression might be prohibited, yet could be permitted were a circumstance to be associated with it. Thus, it is not permissible to say to God—may He be praised and exalted: 'O Sower!' or 'O Cultivator!' while it is permissible to say: 'the one who levels and sows is not the cultivator, but God, the most high and holy One, is the cultivator', or 'the one who scatters the seeds is not the sower, but God Himself is the sower'. So the one who [195] throws is not the thrower, but God Himself is the thrower, as the Most High says: *'it was not you who threw when you threw, but God threw'*.[28] We do not say to God—may He be praised and exalted: 'O humbling One', but we do say: 'O Honourer, O humbling One'. For when they are brought together it is an attribute of praise, for it indicates that the extremities of things are in His hands.[29]

Similarly with prayer: we pray to God—may He be praised and exalted—with His beautiful names as He has commanded us to do, and beyond these names we pray to Him with attributes of praise and glory. So we do not say: 'O existent One', 'O mover', 'O pacifier'. Rather we say: 'O canceller of failings', 'O bestower of blessings', 'O facilitator of all difficulties', and the like. Just as when we address a person, we call him either by his name or by one of the attributes of praise. So we say: 'O noble one', 'O learned one',[30] though we do not say 'O tall one', 'O fair one', unless we are intent upon belittling him. If we were to inquire about his features, we would be told that his complexion is fair and his hair black; but nothing would be mentioned that he would dislike were it to reach him. If it were true, he would not dislike it; only what is thought to be a defect is disliked.

Similarly, if we were to inquire about the One who moves things, stills them, makes them black or white, we would say: he is God—may He be praised and exalted. We do not limit the actions or attributes related to Him to those specifically authorized, since authorization is provided by revelation for whatever is true, unless excepted by unusual circumstances. So God the most high is both existent and originator, the One who manifests and the One who conceals, the One who brings joy and distress, the preserver and destroyer—and it is permissible to apply all these to him, even if they are not mentioned in divine instruction. [196]

If it is said: why is it not permitted to say of God that He is the Knowing One (*al-ʿĀrif*), the Intelligent One (*al-ʿĀqil*), the Clever One (*al-Faṭin*), the Bright One (*al-Dhakī*), and so on, we would say: what forbids these and others like them are the suggestions [of imperfection] associated with them. Whatever contains such suggestions is permissible only with authorization;

as is the case with the Patient (*al-Ṣabūr*), the Mild (*al-Ḥalīm*), and the Merciful One (*al-Raḥīm*). While these contain suggestions [of imperfection], they are nevertheless expressly authorized, whereas the others are not. The suggestion [of imperfection] in 'the intelligent One' (*al-ʿĀqil*) is that his knowledge hobbles him—that is, holds him back, since it is said: 'his intelligence hobbled him'.[31] Moreover, 'cleverness' and 'brightness' convey the speed of perceiving what was concealed from the perceiver, while 'knowledge' conveys a previous state of ignorance. Yet nothing prohibits us from applying any of these terms to God except what we have mentioned [i.e., the suggestion they each convey of imperfection]. So when an expression which does not suggest [any imperfection] at all among those who share a common understanding is taken to be true of God, and when revelation does not expressly forbid it, then we freely permit its being applied to God. And God knows what is right in such matters; He is the source to which we ever return.

# NOTES

## Notes to Part One

[1]In this first approach to their difference, Ghazālī associates name with the predicate, and the thing named with the subject, of a descriptive sentence.

[2]Here name is associated with word (or utterance), act of naming with knowledge, and thing named with the object known.

[3]What Arabic grammarians call 'particles' correspond to our syncategorematic terms: expressions which contribute to the sense of a sentence (as the unit of complete meaning) but which make no sense alone—e.g., prepositions, conjunctions, relative pronouns. The word used (*ḥurūf*) is the same as that for 'letter', suggesting that *particles* are parts of sentences as letters are of words.

[4]The Arabic *ism*, like the Latin *nomen*, can be translated syntactically by 'noun' or semantically by 'name', depending on the context.

[5]By 'agnomen' is meant the *kunya:* it is customary among Arabs to name father and mother by their first-born son preceded by Abū- or Umm- as in: Abū-Yūsuf and Umm-Yūsuf.

[6]Here Ghazālī alludes to an order, among the senses which a term might share—one way of handling equivocal terms whose diverse meanings may be more than accidentally related (cf. note 11).

[7]Ibn Abī Quḥāfa: Abū Bakr, the first Rightly-guided Caliph, also known by the epithet *al-Ṣiddīq*. Cf. *EI* 1.109-11.

[8]That is, practitioners of *Kalām;* cf. note 18.

[9]Aristotle's doctrine of the 'excluded middle' for assertions is alluded to here; as the context elaborates his teaching on direct and indirect predication.

[10]Could this be a negative allusion to the doctrine of atomism commonly accepted among Ashʿarites? In any case Ghazālī's attitude towards this Ashʿarite doctrine is complicated—cf. Lenn Evan Goodman, 'Did al-Ghazālī deny Causality?' *Studia Islamica* 47 (1978), 83-120.

[11]Bukh, Tawḥīd, 12.B; Shurūṭ 3/259.

[12]Two synonymous words for 'lion'.

[13]Reference to a *Ḥadīth Qudsī*, following the translation of William A. Graham, *Divine Word and Prophetic Word in Early Islam* (The Hague: Mouton, 1977), 162. The reference is to a full-length robe girded by an often colourful sash, so that one complements the other for elegance.

[14]'The throne' is a reference to the throne of God—a multi-dimensional symbol in Islamic religious thought.

[15]Although the Arabic term *mushtarak* has many meanings, we are following Harry Wolfson's preferred reading of 'equivocal'—cf. 'Amphibolous Terms in Aristotle, Arabic Philosophy and Maimonides', in *Studies in the History of Philosophy and Religion* I (Cambridge MA: Harvard University Press, 1973) 44-77, esp. 47-73.

[16]Al-Shāfiʿī (d. 204/820) founded a school of jurisprudence, the methodology of which is normally referred to as *Uṣūl*, the word which Ghazālī uses here. The reference, manifestly indirect, should refer to his major work—*Kitāb al-Umm*—but much lore had already developed around his person—cf. *Shorter Encyclopedia of Islam* (Ithaca, NY: Cornell University Press, 1953), 512-15, 613.

[17]The Bedouin reference is two-edged, since their traditional way of life, rooted in early Arabic verse and linguistic habits, made them a repository of the language of the Qur'ān, however unlettered they may have been.

[18]Cf. note 19 below.

[19]Richard McCarthy renders *al-mushāhada* and *al-mukāshafa* (cf. *Freedom and Fulfillment* (Boston: Twayne, 1980) 123 n.55), as 'revelation' and 'direct vision'; Ghazālī contrasts these ways of knowing to that of mere conformity to observance (*taqlīd*).

[20]A traditional definition of *kalām*: 'the science which is concerned with firmly establishing religious beliefs by adducing proofs and with banishing doubts' (cited by Louis Gardet in his contribution to the *Encyclopedia of Islam*, III, 141-50: *ʿilm al-kalām*), catches the spirit of this use of reason in the service of religious beliefs. It is often translated 'theology', in contradistinction to *fiqh* ('jurisprudence'), yet Ibn Khaldūn locates it with *fiqh* among the 'traditional sciences', indicating that its use of reason is more apologetic than inquiring. See Harry A. Wolfson, *Philosophy of the Kalam* (Cambridge, MA: Harvard University Press, 1976) 3-43.

[21]After its introduction by al-Nūrī (d. 907), it was especially al-Ḥallāj who drew out the implications of *ʿishq* ('passionate love') in relation to God (Schimmel, 60,72,137). It was opposed by some of the 'orthodox', whose preference for *maḥabba* enjoyed Qur'ānic support (V:54), and who understandably found difficul-

ties with the reference to passion. Yet Ḥallāj's use of *ʿishq* is what links him most closely to western mystics—cf. Anawati-Gardet, 8,103.

[22]An allusion to the place of the sheikh in the Sufi orders, whose successor inherited his carpet—cf. Schimmel, 236. For the sense of 'close' *(qurb)*, see Schimmel, 132-33. The 'carpet' is also the sitting place of the king's inner circle of intimates in ancient Mid-East tradition.

[23]An allusion to Ghazālī's conviction that God has created the world in the 'best way possible'—cf. Eric Ormsby, *Theodicy in Islamic Thought* (Princeton, NJ: Princeton University Press, 1984).The 'specifying mark of divinity' reflects Ibn Sīnā, *al-Shifā'*, 8.4: 'There is no quiddity for the necessary existent other than the fact that it is necessary existent'—cf. Avicenne, *La Metaphysique* (Bks 6-10), trans. G.C. Anawati (Paris: Vrin, 1985); everything else is defined as that 'whose existence is possible'.

[24]Al-Junayd (d. 910) was credited with directing many early Sufi masters, among whom was al-Ḥallāj. He was notable for his balance and sobriety, which state he placed above 'intoxication'. Though he recognized that the requisite loss of self *(fanā')* may require ecstatic experiences, it was a 'second sobriety' which confirmed one's 'remaining' *(baqā')* in God—cf. Schimmel, 57-9, Anawati-Gardet, 34-5.

[25]Dhu'l-Nūn (d.859), of Nubian parents and Coptic stock, lived in Egypt, where his access to Neoplatonic influences gave his writings a philosophical turn—cf. Schimmel, 42-47; Anawati-Gardet, 27. This incident is also mentioned in Ghazālī's *Iḥyā'*, *Kitāb Dhikr al-mawt*, trans. Winter, 91.

[26]The two extreme treatments of divine attributes in Islam are represented by those who utterly deny their appropriateness *(taʿṭīl)* and those who take the descriptive Qur'ānic texts at face value: *tashbīh* (anthropomorphism). The motives for denial were philosophical, lest a multiplicity of attributes undermine divine simplicity, yet one may deny the reality of attributes in divinity without calling their appropriateness into question, so a range of intermediate positions can be found among actual religious thinkers in Islam. Cf. Louis Gardet and Georges Anawati, *Introduction à la Théologie Musulmane* (Paris: Vrin, 1968), 56-58; *Shorter Encyclopedia of Islam: taʿṭīl, tashbīh*, 583-85.

[27]See note 7 above.

[28]From a *Ḥadīth Qudsī* ('Divine Saying'): God said: 'I have prepared for my upright servants what neither eye has seen, nor ear has heard, nor has entered into the heart of [any] man'—translation of William A. Graham,

*Divine Word and Prophetic Word in Early Islām.* Christians will hear echoes of the New Testament: I Corinthians II:9, itself 'a free combination of Isaiah LXIV:3 and Jeremiah III:16, or possibly a quotation from the *Apocalypse of Elijah*' (Jerusalem Bible).

[29]The 'knowers' is a Sufi allusion to a manner of knowing God by a certain familiarity. The parallels with Maimonides and Aquinas are palpable: cf. *Guide of the Perplexed*, I:58: 'Glory then to Him who is such that when the intellects contemplate His essence, their apprehension turns into incapacity..., and when tongues aspire to magnify Him by means of attributive qualifications, all eloquence turns into weariness and incapacity!' (trans. Shlomo Pines, Chicago: University of Chicago Press, 1963); and *Exposito super librum Boethii de Trinitate* I.II.I: 'Since our understanding finds itself knowing God most perfectly when it knows that the divine nature lies beyond whatever it can apprehend in our present state, we can be said to know God as unknown, once we sum up what knowledge we have of Him' (ed. Decker, Leiden, 1959).

[30]Muslim: Ṣalāt, 222.

[31]Al-Shāfiʿī (767-820) is the founder of the Shāfiʿī school of law, and al-Muzanī was an early disciple; cf. *Shorter Encyclopedia of Islam* 512-15.

[32]The text here is ambiguous as between the subjective genitive: 'God's knowledge' and the objective genitive: 'the knowledge [we have] of God', and the ambiguity is heightened by variant readings: cf. Shehadi 56 n.3. We have altered his paragraph separation at this point for clarity of sense.

[33]'Light from light' is a favourite Sufi metaphor, which favours an emanationist, if not a pantheistic, metaphysics. Though Ghazālī adopts it here, and even more so in his *Mishkāt al-Anwār* (*Le Tabernacle des Lumières*, trad. Roger Deladrière [Paris: Seuil, 1981]), he specifies the 'source of existence' as distinct from its radiation in this text.

[34]See his comments on *al-Ḥaqq* ('The Truth', no.52) for the sense in which only God truly exists.

[35]A celebrated Qur'ānic verse referring to the Prophet's actions at the battle of Badr, where the first Muslim victory became on reflection their 'Exodus event'—cf. W. Montgomery Watt, *Muḥammad: Prophet and Statesman* (Oxford: Oxford University Press, 1961), 125-26.

# Notes to Part Two

[1]Muslim, Dhikr, 6.

[2]Reading *muqsiṭ*, rather than *muqassiṭ* (as in Shehadi).

[3]A nearly verbatim allusion to the famous verse: *'everything is perishing except His face'* (XXVIII:88).

[4]The word which we shall render as 'aspiration'—*himma*—denotes a 'spiritual ambition', which the Sufis, like the desert monks, linked with a 'holy competitiveness' among those desiring to come closer to God (cf. also note 92).

[5]Bukhārī, Anṣār 5/53; Muslim 4/1766, Tir. 5/14.

[6]The best test of this observation is one's response to a beggar: we often give something to relieve ourselves of their demanding presence, especially when they may be disfigured.

[7]Another way of distinguishing them is only suggested by this sentence: *al-Raḥmān* refers to God's essential goodness, 'before creation' (as it were), while *al-Raḥīm* refers to God's response to creation. It is to capture that difference, as well as to avoid synonymy, that we have eschewed Arberry's now classical rendering: 'the Merciful, the Compassionate', in favour of 'the Infinitely Good, the Merciful'. But see Gimaret, 375-82.

[8]*Ḥadīth Qudsī*; Graham 184 (Saying 59, iii: Han. II, 313); Bukh, Tawḥīd 9/153.

[9]Cupping: a procedure using a heated receptacle to draw blood from punctured veins by creating a partial vacuum.

[10]One thinks how easily some philosophers hypothesize 'possible worlds' without attending to the subtle interdependencies which may (or may not) be demanded for something to be the case.

[11]The word rendered 'revelation' here is *al-sharʿ*: the basis for the *sharīʿa* or rule of life proper to Islam, and since that basis is revealed, the rendering seems *a propos*. Not only the Qur'ān but also the *ḥadīth*—sayings attributed to Muḥammad—constitute this basis.

[12]Ghazālī develops this allegory at length in his *Iḥyā' ʿUlūm al-Dīn*, Bk. 21 (McCarthy, Appendix V, pp. 368-72).

[13]Preferring God to God's promised rewards is a common Sufi refrain, often taken to paradoxical lengths, to emphasize a disinterested love for God.

[14]Literally, 'enclosure of holiness' = paradise.

[15]Cf. Qur'ān, XXVI:89.

[16]Muslim, Īmān, 24.

[17]Islam both requires and assures *salām* (well-being); 'speech

or actions': literally, 'tongue or hand'. 'His lower self renders *nafsihi*—cf. note 25. The one who is *flawless* also *protects* others from being harmed; this name is ambiguous as between an essential attribute and one of action—cf. Gimaret, 204-5.

[18]*Ḥadīth Qudsī*—cf. *al-Mughnī*, I, 149 (2).

[19]Muslim, Īmān 73/83.

[20]Ibn Ḥanbal I, 390; Bukhārī, Riqāq 26.

[21]'Ancient writings'(or 'books') refers to the Hebrew or Christian scriptures; the reference here is to the apocryphal Gospel of Barnabas.

[22]Maj, Zuhd 37.

[23]*Zuhd* (renunciation) refers concretely to those Sufi practices designed to open the heart to God, and the sign of being on the right track is to renounce all rewards, including that of paradise—cf. Schimmel, 110. Otherwise it is a mere strategy and hardly praiseworthy because it does not succeed in re-aligning base desires.

[24]Cf. Qur'ān XXIII: 12-14 for a description of the creation of man which serves well to guide this account, and XV:26 for insisting on the kind of clay used.

[25]According to this principle, elaborated in Part One, an ever greater appreciation of the traces of the Creator is open to us.

[26]This inversion with respect to divine and human knowing is basic to the philosophies attendant upon a creation-tradition: God does not apprehend objects as we do; God's knowledge brings them into being.

[27]Suyūṭī, cf. *n. f. ḥ;* Ṭabarānī, *al-Muʿjam al-kabīr* 19/234.

[28]cf. Qur'ān, XXV:70.

[29]Han IV, 159; Bukh, Maẓālim 3.

[30]This Sufi meaning of soul (*nafs*) is not the philosophical 'principle of life', but 'the lower self, the base instincts, what we might render in the biblical sense as 'the flesh' (Schimmel 112-16).

[31]This discussion of pure or 'disinterested' love of God is central to Sufism—see A. Schimmel's remarks on Rābiʿa, the early woman Sufi saint (38-41).

[32]The 'black-and-white-eyed ones', or houris, epitomize the sensual pleasures of paradise: cf. *Encyclopedia of Islam* III, 581-82 (*ḥūr*); II, 447-52 (*djanna*).

[33]Ḥātim al-Aṣamm is Abū ʿAbd al-Raḥmān Ḥātim ibn ʿAnwān ibn Yūsuf, a renowned Sufi shaykh—cf. Sulamī, *Ṭabaqāt al-Ṣufiya* (Leiden: Brill, 1960).

[34]Mus, Zakāt 79.

[35]Reading *ʿabd* for *ʿahd*.

[36]Desert travel is customarily at night.

[37]Reading *ʿabd* for *ʿahd*.

[38]This pair of names was employed by Sufis to mark the stations of *fear* and *hope* along the way to proximity with God—cf. Schimmel 128-9.

[39]Mus, Īmān, 379.

[40]*Hadīth Qudsī*—cf. Graham 173, where a similar saying (in negative form) can be found.

[41]'Religious exercises and battles' may sound to Christian ears like an odd conjunction and set of priorities, yet as Fazlur Rahman underscores, 'Muḥammad... was *duty-bound* to succeed' in his mission, and so was called to undertake all ethically sound means that were necessary (*Islam*, 7-9).

[42]This is Ghazālī's adaptation of Ibn Sīnā's dividing all that exists into (1) what is necessary in itself (God) and (2) what is possible in itself, yet rendered necessary by reason of its necessary emanation from the One (*al-Shifā'* 1.6; English translation in Arthur Hyman and James Walsh, eds., *Philosophy in the Middle Ages*, 2nd ed. (Indianapolis, IN: Hackett, 1983) 241-44. Ghazālī transfers the reason for the second 'existential' necessity to the decree of a free creator, using the metaphor of a pen to compare God's creating with composing the Qur'ān, as the Qur'ān itself does (cf. XVIII:110, XXXI:27).

[43]Mus, Qadar 7.

[44]The word we have translated 'vision' here—*shuhūd*—is a variant for *shahāda*, the Muslim formula for God's uniqueness, which the Sufis insisted could not be uttered authentically without God's being present to the believer, so Anawati and Gardet translate it 'testimonial presence' (128)—cf. Schimmel, 267.

[45]Reading *ya'baqu* with L and T (Shehadi 105 n. 5); the first part of this sentence freely adapts sura LXVII:3-4 to the context, borrowing extensively from its language.

[46]Exploiting, as Ghazālī does, the ambiguities in *ism* (noun, name) and *af'āl* (actions, verbs).

[47]The image here is similar to Plato's god for a human inquiry: 'to find the true joints in reality', that is, the way it is put together.

[48]Reading the variant *ḥakīm*; one could also render it as 'He is *arbitrator* insofar as He plans things', following Shehadi's principal text, *ḥakam*.

[49]Gimaret notes that *'aẓīm* is seldom used of physical objects, hence the English 'tremendous' alludes to Otto's *tremendum*.

[50]Reading *'abd* for *'ahd*.

[51]Tir., Birr 35.

[52]This is Book 32, the second book in Volume IV of Ghazālī's masterwork seeking to accommodate Sufi practices and Sunni observance. Portions of the *Iḥyā'* have been translated into English, but not this book, unfortunately, because it gives an extended treatment of *grace* in a Muslim context. For a German translation see R. Gramlich, *Muḥammad al-Ghazālīs Lehre von den Stufen zur Gottesliebe* (Wiesbaden: Franz Steiner Verlag, 1984) 139-293.

[53]Those thinkers who tended to interpret anthropomorphic verses in the Qur'ān and the tra-

dition in a crudely literal way—cf. *Encyclopedia of Islam* III.269.

[54]Reading *yuʿabbaru* rather than *yuʿayyaru*, as Shehadi has it (120, final line).

[55]Ghazālī tends to call the traditions which go back to Muḥammad *akhbār* (sing., *khabar*), which we have rendered 'report'. Cf. *Encyclopedia of Islam* IV. 895a.

[56]Ghazālī interprets *ḥasīb* (literally, 'one who reckons') in the sense of *kāfī* ('one who suffices'); for other understandings, see Gimaret, 261-62. The current sense is of 'one esteemed'.

[57]Utilizing the variant reading in Shehadi, 125 n.3.

[58]Ghazālī and all religious thinkers must deal with the illusion of *autonomy*, which he treats here under the rubric of *sufficiency*. Operating from a different tradition and optic, Aquinas was said by Chesterton to be concerned with 'defending the independence of dependent things'.

[59]A celebrated contention of Sufis, initiated by Rābiʿa; cf. A. Schimmel 38-9; Anawati and Gardet 166-68.

[60]Utilizing the variant reading, 126 n. 2.

[61]*Iḥyā'* IV, Book 36 (Bousquet 395-407), French translation: Marie-Louise Siauve, *L'amour de Dieu chez Gazali* (Paris: Vrin, 1986).

[62]Shehadi's variants(128n. 1,2) would allow one to begin the sentence: 'Man may adorn himself by acquiring these qualities. . . '. In either case, the expression *fī* (or *bi*) *iktisāb* is a quasi-technical one, noting that creatures are so qualified only 'by acquisition'.

[63]Mus, Alfāẓ 10.

[64]Bukh, Nikāḥ 73; Muslim, Nikāḥ 104.

[65]An allusion to XVIII:110: 'Say: Though the sea became ink for the words of my Lord, verily the sea would be used up before the words of my Lord were exhausted. . .'

[66]No text locatable; see *al-Mughnī* IV 140 #3; mentioned in al-ʿAjalawnī, *Kashf al-khafā'*, I.507.

[67]Maj. Zuhd 31.

[68]Han. V 197.

[69]Maj. 9.

[70]Ibid., 24.

[71]No text locatable, but mentioned in al-Hindī, *Kanz al-ʿummāl* XVI/699.

[72]Tir., Zuhd 11.

[73]Maj., Muqaddima 7.

[74]Su., under ḥ k m.

[75]Su., under q n'.

[76]Su., under s b r.

[77]Han., 1441, see *al-Mughnī* III 61 n.1; p. 251 n.1.

[78]Han., IV 148.

[79]Tir. Qiyāma, 6.

[80]Mus, Jannah 77, see also Ibn Isḥāq, *Sīrat Rasūl Allāh*, 454 (English translation: A. Guillaume, *The Life of Muḥammad* [Karachi: Oxford University Press, 1986] 306).

[81]The term *amr* is ambigous between 'command' and 'matter' or 'thing'; cf. *Iḥyā'* III, 1; McCarthy 366, 377.

[82]As this sentence indicates, and the following corroborates, *al-Ḥaqq* can also be read as 'the Real', since that is most true which most truly exists. The ambiguity is fruitful, however, rather than misleading, as can be confirmed by interchanging 'real' with 'true' in what follows. A coherent translation seemed to require verbal consistency, however.

[83]That is al-Ḥallāj—cf. note 97 below.

[84]'. . . they cite Him as witness for Himself'—an allusion, perhaps, to *waḥdat al-shuhūd*, or 'unity of witnessing', whereby the only authentic witness to the oneness of God is that which the One makes in and through us. It represents the more orthodox alternative to *waḥdat al-wujūd*, or 'unity of existing', which would represent the obvious reading of al-Ḥallāj's celebrated confession—the one which Ghazālī here (and later) assiduously avoids.

[85]An allusion to the practice of *dhikr*, the continuous repetition of the name(s) of God, a practice central to sufism—cf. Schimmel 167-78, Anawati-Gardet 187-234.

[86]This is the distinction between *essence* and *existence* made by Ibn Sīnā to bring Aristotle's scheme of substance into a world-view dominated by One from whom all existing things emanate. And as the following paragraph testifies, the same distinction offered him and Ghazālī a way of uniquely characterizing that One as well: the only one whose essence is to exist. Cf. my 'Essence and Existence: Avicenna and Greek Philosophy', MIDEO (*Mélanges de l'Institut Dominicain d'Études Orientales*) 17 (1986) 53-66.

[87]*Al-Ṣamad* is rendered by Pickthall: 'the eternally Besought' (CXII:2). Its meaning is particularly elusive (cf. Gimaret, 320-23); it has also the sense of one who prevails, who stays through it all. For a special application to non-violent resistance, see Raja Shehadeh, *Samed: Journal of a West Bank Palestinian* (New York: Adama, 1984).

[88]Nearly all of the terms in this sentence are Sufi allusions: *sulūk* ('wayfaring'), *manāzil* ('stages', literally 'resting places which mark stages along the way'), all of which pertains to the 'knowers' (*ʿārifūn*)—see Schimmel 98,340; Anawati-Gardet 127.

[89]No text locatable.

[90]For Abū Yazīd, see note 100.

[91]Maj, Zuhd 2.

[92]This is the famous 'best possible' teaching of Ghazālī regarding the world as it has been created by God—cf. Eric Ormsby, *Theodicy in Islamic Thought* (Princeton, NJ: Princeton University Press, 1984).

[93]Literally, 'king in the kingdom of his soul according to the measure of power given to it [i.e., his soul]', which would sound strange since his *body* has been introduced as the kingdom, yet this easy transition could be evidence that Ghazālī holds a more holistic view of the person than does Ibn Sīnā, and this would accord with his orthodoxy on the resurrection.

[94]Al-Ḥākim al-Naysābūrī, *al-Mustadrak*, Ahwāl IV/576.

[95]In short, Ghazālī is warning against an Ashʿarite temptation to over-react in defending the reality of attributes in God, over against the Muʿtazilite denial of attributes in defence of divine simplicity. A sign of over-reaction would be to hypostatize the attributes and so reduplicate the consideration of God *via* His attributes with a consideration of the attributes themselves.

[96]No text, but cf. *al-Mughnī* IV, 307, n. 6; 316, n. 1; mentioned in Haythamī, *Majmaʿ al-zawā'id*, Īmān I.36.

[97]The verbal noun *ittiḥād* comes from the verb 'to make one' in one of its derived forms. Hence it can be translated 'identification' (so Anawati-Gardet) or 'union' (Schimmel). We will sometimes render it 'assimilation' where the context specifies that the assimilation is one of identification. It is occasionally used to signify the goal of the Sufi journey, along with *ittiṣāl* ('arriving')—cf. Anawati-Gardet 53-54, *passim*. *Ḥulūl*, which we have rendered in a more neutral philosophical idiom as 'inherence', is rendered by Schimmel by the more evocative 'indwelling', and may also be given a theological sense close to 'incarnation'. We have avoided the latter term lest Christian connotations invade Islamic thought-forms here, yet Ḥallāj's use may well bear Christian overtones—cf. *Encylopedia of Islam*, *ḥulūl*; and Louis Massignon, *The Passion of Al-Hallaj*, trans. Herbert Mason (Princeton, NJ: Princeton University Press, 1986), *passim*.

[98]The phrase 'creator of the heavens and the earth and all that is between them' is typically Qur'ānic (e.g., V:17), thereby specifying mankind as God's vicars (cf. VII:69) standing as we do 'between heaven and earth'.

[99]Literally, 'he is he': a handy shorthand for the formula of identity, as we saw earlier, yet in the next paragraph it will be preferable to render it literally.

[100]A celebrated statement of Abū Yazīd (Bayezid) Bisṭāmī (d. 874), whose 'theopathic locutions' [*shaṭaḥāt*] were designed, like Zen koans, to startle one into consciousness of the paradoxes inherent in self-knowledge as a path to union—cf. Schimmel 47-50; Anawati-Gardet 32-3,110-15.

[101]A celebrated statement of al-Ḥallāj (858-922), the most famous mystic of Baghdad and of

early Sufism—cf. Schimmel 62-77; Anawati-Gardet 35-40, 107-10. For an extended treatment, cf. Massignon (note 97).

[102] A classic Arabic verse—cf. Schimmel 353, for a later Sufi use.

[103] Cf. Schimmel, 49.

[104] The expressions 'on the way' [*sālik*] and 'arrived' [*wāṣil*] embody the dynamic tension of the Sufi journey to God—cf. Schimmel 98, 105, 423; 148; and Anawati-Gardet 42.

[105] The term which we have rendered 'determination' (or 'striving')—*himma*—might also be translated 'zeal' or 'spiritual energy', and is often linked to a shaykh's power—cf. Schimmel 79, 257; Anawati-Gardet's rendering of 'sustained attention' evokes Simone Weil.

[106] For a view of the role of ritual purity [*ṭahāra*] in Sufi thought and life, see Schimmel 148-49.

[107] 'The word usually translated as "saint" [*walī*] means "someone who is under special protection, friend"' (Schimmel, 199), so we have rendered its abstract form by 'friendship' as a reminder that the saints are considered to be 'friends of God'. It is generally considered to be the ultimate stage, except for those who are specially singled out to be prophets, and notably *the* Prophet.

[108] Lest the switch in examples to matters of Islamic faith lead the reader to presume that Ghazālī is mixing two levels of discourse here, it is useful to note that he proceeds in an orderly fashion: one who failed to abide by reason in the sense of swallowing contradictions would thereby be unable to distinguish true from false, and thus could incline towards believing false—not self-contradictory—things about the *sharīʿa.* And were such a one to make light of the power of reason (displayed in spotting contradictions) in his own defense, he would be failing to discern the difference between reason and faith, and in practice such a one is no better than one who fails to recognize contradictions, and so comes under Aristotle's stricture: he is beneath discourse.

[109] Ghazālī is responding here to a convention of his tradition which had made a canonical list of seven attributes to mark divinity: life, knowledge, power, will, hearing, seeing, and speaking (cf. Chapter 3 of this Part). The accepted list is that of Abū Manṣūr al-Baghdādī—cf. Gimaret 107-13. These are clearly intended as essential attributes of God, and hence non-relational; applicable even 'before creation', as it were.

[110] Ghazālī is less than orderly here; indeed one suspects he finds this exercise tedious and pointless. The numbering we have used corresponds to the exposition which follows.

[111] Whereas Ghazālī's commentary itself put *al-Raḥmān* [the In-

finitely Good] closest to Allāh, here he cedes to Sufi predilections for *al-Ḥaqq*.

[112]A clear allusion to the manner of revelation of the Qur'ān, where divine wisdom must take on human speech.

[113]If creation is to be explicated as 'necessary emanation', as the Islamic philosophers were wont to do, *will* must be reduced to zero.

[114]A classic formula of the philosophers, stemming from Aristotle and articulated by al-Fārābī in a crucial argument in *al-Madīna al-Fāḍila: Al-Fārābī on the Perfect State*, ed. Richard Walzer (Oxford: Clarendon Press, 1985) Ch. 1, par. 6 (pp. 71-3).

[115]This reference to creation as emanation continues Ghazālī's exposition of the position of the philosophers; he is not asserting it in his own name.

[116]*Tahāfut al-Falāsifa*, whose best rendering is that wholly contained within Averroes' refutation: *Averroes' Tahāfut al-Tahāfut*, trans. Simon van den Bergh (Oxford: Oxford University Press, 1954).

## Notes to Part Three

[1]Giving a different translation of the same letters than *al-Malik* in the list used in this commentary, although *al-Hādī* and *al-Nūr* are included in the list which is used in this commentary even though Ghazālī places them here among the alternates.

[2]Da., Adab 9.

[3]Maj., Zuhd 37, Tawḥīd 12.

[4]Maj., Duʿā' 10.B

[5]Al-Bayhaqī, *al-Sunan al-Kubrā*, Ṣiyam IV.201; see *al-Mughnī* 1.93 n. 1.

[6]Han. 1.391.

[7]Han. 1.391, 456.

[8]On 'the greatest name', see Schimmel 25, and 177: 'The Greatest Name is hidden, but many a mystic has claimed that he possesses it and that it enables him to perform every kind of miracle'. Ghazālī, as we shall see, is intent on demystifying it. Cf. Gimaret, 85-94, for a survey of views.

[9]The Arabic name for the Queen of Sheba, cf. *Encyclopedia of Islam* 1.1219; Āṣaf [Ibn Barakhyā] was the alleged *wazīr* of Solomon (1.686).

[10]Tir., Daʿawāt 5.517.

[11]Maj., Duʿā' 9.

[12]Han. 2.258.

[13]*Musnad* is a technical term denoting a ḥadīth collection arranged according to names of transmitters; Abū ʿĪsā al-Tirmidhī (d. 884/889) is author of one of the collections of ḥadīth (usually termed *sunan*), notable for its

critical examination of the *isnāds*. Among Aḥmad al-Bayhaqī's major collections is one entitled *al-Sunan al-Kubrā* (cf. *EI* 1.1130).

[14]These are technical terms in *ḥadīth: gharīb* commonly refers to an authentic account which rests on the authority of only one Companion of the Prophet, while *isnād* refers to the list of attestors.

[15]The famous ʿAlī ibn Ḥazm (994-1064) was from Cordoba and spent his life in Andalusia. Although a traditionist, the bulk of his work was legal, literary and philosophical, notably concerning divine attributes (cf. *EI* 3.790-99). *Ijtihād* is a technical term in legal matters, meaning the kind of judgment which an individual versed in such matters could take upon himself.

[16]Mus. Dhikr 5

[17]We translate *tawqīf* as 'divine instruction', referring to the teaching proceeding both from the Qur'ān and the *ḥadīth*—cf. Gimaret, 42-6. We shall regularly distinguish *sharʿ* from *sharīʿa* by rendering *sharʿ* 'revelation', since its primary reference is the Qur'ān; and *sharīʿa* 'divine law', since it encompasses the body of judgments flowing from the Qur'ān for the direction of the community.

[18]Qāḍī Abū-Bakr (d. 1013), also known as al-Bāqillānī, was a major figure in systematising Ash'arism; cf. *EI* 1.958-59.

[19]Abu'l-Ḥasan al-Ashʿarī (873-936) was the founder of the school of Islamic religious thought which bean his name, and which had replaced the Muʿtazilite school as the dominant *kalām* school before the time of Ghazālī, although Ghazālī's staunch support of this school helped confirm its authoritative status.

[20]The Arabic term *ism* shares with the Latin term *nomen* the grammatical meaning of 'noun' as well as the semantic meaning of 'name', with the further ambiguity that 'noun' can also mean 'verbal noun' or 'adjective'. We shall render *ism* as the context demands.

[21]We have translated *bayḍ* (literally 'white') as 'fair' to render the passage more faithfully to the connotations of *bayḍ* in this context. To grasp the point of Ghazālī's allusion here, we must think of nicknames given someone according to their physical characteristics, like 'stretch' or 'whitey'.

[22]Qāsim means 'one who divides', and Jāmiʿ 'one who unites'.

[23]We generally render *dall* as 'indicate', but here it seemed appropriate to use the more modern expression 'refer', without presuming, however, the modern distinction of *sense* from *reference*. Medievals used some variant of 'signify' to convey both, so Ghazālī must make his use of *dall* precise in this context.

[24]So-called *iḍāfa*-constructions in Arabic allow one to juxtapose

two nouns so that one modifies the other, as in 'servant of the king', and there are specific grammatical rules for forming the plural of the construction, as in 'mother-in-law'. Cf. J.A. Haywood and H.M. Nahmad, *A New Arabic Grammar* (London: Lund Humphries, 1965) Ch. 8.

[25]The first two names allude to the Prophet as one eminently worthy of praise, while the others could be rendered: God-fearing (*al-Muttaqī*), Forgiving one (*al-Māḥī*), The Final One *(al-ʿĀqib)*, Prophet of repentance *(Nabī al-Tawba)*, Prophet of mercy (*Nabī al-Raḥmah*), Prophet of war (*Nabī al-Malḥama*). This quotation comes from Tir., Adab 67; Muslim, Faḍā'il 4.

[26]Using analogous cases to clarify the scope and meaning of *sharīʿa* is a standard procedure in Islamic jurisprudence, known as *qiyās*—cf. *Shorter Encyclopedia of Islam*, 266-67.

[27]We render 'except incidentally' by 'extenuating (or unusual) circumstances', since in the context of the application of law, general rules must be open to exception in the light of unforeseen circumstances.

[28]Sura VIII:17. For the context, see W.M. Watt (n. 35 of Pt. One).

[29]An allusion to the reach of God's power, as one who can reconcile opposites.

[30]The best rendering for *faqīh* would be 'jurisprudent'—one learned in law, but economy of English expression demands the simpler 'O learned one'. For Ghazālī's concern about belittling someone, see note 21.

[31]Ghazālī exploits the ambiguity of the verb *ʿaqal*, one of whose meanings is 'to tie' and especially 'to hobble' a camel; and he finds this ambiguity displayed in a proverbial saying.

# INDEX OF DIVINE NAMES

(List of Names on pages 49 to 51)

# INDEX OF PERSONS

# Bibliography


HADITH REFERENCES

Abū Dāwud, *Sunan*, ed. Muḥammad Muḥyī'd Dīn ʿAbd al-Ḥamīd, Cairo, 1935, 4 vols. [ = Da.]

Al-Bukhārī, *Ṣaḥīḥ*, ed. L. Krehl and Th. W. Juynboll, Leiden, 1862-1908, 4 vols. [ = Bukh.]

Ibn Ḥanbal, *Musnad*, Cairo, 1313, 6 vols. [ = Han.]

Ibn Māja, *Sunan*, ed. Muḥammad Fu'ād ʿAbd Al-Bāqī, Cairo, 1952-53, 2 vols. [ = Maj.]

Muslim, *Ṣaḥīḥ*, ed. Muḥammad Fu'ād ʿAbd al-Bāqī, Cairo, 1955-56, 5 vols. [ = Mus.]

Al-Suyūṭī, *Fayḍ al-Qādir sharḥ al-Jāmiʿ aṣ-ṣaghīr*, Cairo, 1938, 6 vols. [ = Su.]

Al-Tirmidhī, *al-Jāmiʿ aṣ-Ṣaḥīḥ*, ed. Aḥmad Muḥammad Shākir (vol. 1, 2) Muḥammad Fu'ād ʿAbd al-Bāqī (vol 3) Ibrāhīm ʿAṭwa ʿIwaḍ (vols 4, 5), Cairo, 1937-65 [ =Tir.]

AL-GHAZALI

*Al-Maqṣad al-asnā fī sharḥ maʿānī asmā' Allāh al-ḥusnā*, ed. Fadlou A. Shehadi (Beyrouth: Dar El-Machreq, 1971).

Bousquet, G.-H. *Iḥya ʿOuloūm ed-Dīn, ou Vivification des Sciences de la Foi, analyse et index*. (Paris: Besson, 1955).

*Iḥyā ʿulūm al-dīn*, 4 vols., Cairo, 1928.

McCarthy, Richard, *Freedom and Fulfillment* (Boston: Twayne, 1980)—containing portions of the *Maqṣad* in translation in Appendix IV.

*Ninety-nine Names of God in Islam*, translation of Part II of the *Maqṣad* by Robert Stade (Ibadan, Nigeria: Daystar Press, 1970).

REFERENCE WORKS

Anawati, G.-C. and Gardet, Louis, *Mystique Musulmane* (Paris: Vrin, 1986).

*Encyclopedia of Islam*, 2nd edition (Leiden: E.J. Brill, 1983).

*Shorter Encyclopedia of Islam* (Ithaca, NY: Cornell University Press, 1974).

Gimaret, Daniel, *Les noms divins en Islam* (Paris: Cerf, 1988).

Graham, William A., *Divine Word and Prophetic Word in Early Islam* (The Hague: Mouton, 1977).

Jabre, Farid, *Essai sur le lexique de Ghazali* (Beyrouth: Publications de l'Université Libanaise, 1970).
Kazimirski, A. de B., *Dictionnaire Arabe-Francais* (Paris: Maisonneuve, 1860).
Rahman, Fazlur, *Islam* (London: Weidenfeld and Nicolson, 1967).
Schimmel, Annemarie, *Mystical Dimensions of Islam* (Chapel Hill, NC:University of North Carolina Press, 1976).

# GENERAL INDEX

accident (*ʿaraḍ*), 16, 156
*ʿadam, see* non-existence
*amn, see* security
angels, 33, 71, 82, 103, 104, 109, 133
animals, 71, 82, 103, 108, 142
anthropomorphism, 90
*ʿaraḍ, see* accident
arrival/on the way (*wāṣil/sālik*), 156, 157
attributes (*ṣifāt*), 15–19, 37, 40–45, 161

caliph, 66
cause (*sabab*), 86–94, 103, 144
common noun, 28
contradiction, 17
creation, 68, 121

determination (*himma*), 156
*dhāt, see* essence
disclosure, 80
divine decree, 57, 86–91
divine instruction (*tawqīf*), 3, 64, 177, 180
divine law, 179
divine unity (*tawḥīd*), 25, 148

equivocal terms, 29
essence (*dhāt*), 14, 15, 37, 131, 160
essential reality (*ḥaqīqa*), 6, 13, 14, 31, 41, 45
eternal, eternity, 19, 20, 105, 115, 121, 124, 146
evil (*sharr*), 55, 56, 61, 144

existence (*wujūd*), 6, 19, 51, 59, 65, 68, 105, 106, 124, 129, 130, 134, 136, 139, 145, 146
expression, 6–8

faith (*taṣdīq*), 27
form (*ṣūra*), 7, 71

*ḥaqīqa, see* essential reality
heart, 80, 98, 109, 112, 114, 140, 142, 154
heavenly kingdom (*malakūt*), 79, 98
*himma, see* determination
holiness, 121
*ḥulūl, see* inherence

identification (*ittiḥād*), 149–155
identity/difference, 5, 6, 9, 13, 17
*ʿilm, see* knowledge
individual, 6
inherence (*ḥulūl*), 149, 155–158
*ittiḥād, see* identification

*jawhar, see* substance

knower, 42, 59, 67, 76, 134
knowledge (*ʿilm*), 6, 60, 79–81, 98, 114–117, 123–126, 129, 142, 164, 165

likeness, 6, 34, 36, 39, 45
literal/metaphorical, 72

*māhiyya, see* quiddity
*malakūt, see* heavenly kingdom